THE WORLD ALMANAC OF FIRST LADIES

Also by Lu Ann Paletta

The World Almanac of Presidential Facts
(with Fred L. Worth)

THE WORLD ALMANAC® OF

FIRST LADIES

LU ANN PALETTA

WORLD ALMANAC
AN IMPRINT OF PHAROS BOOKS • A SCRIPPS HOWARD COMPANY
NEW YORK

For Trees—Because the Phantom asked me to

First published in 1990.

Library of Congress Cataloging-in-Publication Data

Paletta, Lu Ann.
    The world almanac of first ladies / Lu Ann Paletta
p. cm.
    Sequel to: The world almanac of presidential facts.
    ISBN 0-88687-587-0 : $21.95.—ISBN 0-88687-586-2 (pbk.): $9.95
1. Presidents--United States--Wives--Miscellanea. 2. Presidents-
  -United States--Wives--Humor. I. Title.
E176.2.P35 1990
973'.0992--dc20
[B]   89-78438
                                         CIP

Printed in the United States of America

World Almanac
An Imprint of Pharos Books
A Scripps Howard Company
200 Park Avenue
New York, NY 10166

10 9 8 7 6 5 4 3 2 1

CONTENTS

PREFACE

This book is a tribute to those women who have held the most demanding, strenuous, and exciting job in America—First Lady. The president's wife (or his hostess) has no official job. She is not elected, and she has no legislative powers. Yet, to the president she can be as valuable as a thousand astute politicians. She is his best goodwill ambassador both here and abroad; she can subtly influence his actions with a power Congress can only envy.

Prior to the beginning of this century, First Ladies were usually homemakers who believed their key role was to be a wife and mother. She was only seen at social events and, with few exceptions, never became involved in political affairs. But all that changed in 1902 when the new First Lady, Edith Carow Roosevelt, hired a social secretary to keep up with increasing demands on her time. The role of the president's wife had changed from homemaker and hostess to that of a public wife.

Ellen Wilson was the first to have an official "cause" when she advocated better housing in the slums around Washington. But it was Eleanor Roosevelt, whose tireless support of numerous pet projects, made it almost a necessity for the First Lady to espouse causes. First Ladies were now expected to campaign for their husbands, give speeches, and travel on their own. The office of First Lady was born.

Independent reporter Mary Clemmer Ames is generally credited with first using the term in print. In covering the 1877 inauguration of Ohioan Rutherford B. Hayes, she referred to his wife Lucy Webb Hayes as "First Lady of the Land." The term came into popular use after Charles Nirdlinger's play about Dolley Madison, *The First Lady in the Land*, opened in 1911.

The term, however, had been used earlier, on at least two occasions. During the Civil War, British journalists called Varina Howell Davis, wife of the president of the Confederacy, the "First Lady of the South." Emily Edson Briggs, in her book, *The Olivia Letters,* about Washington social affairs during the Reconstruction Era, used the term to describe Julia Dent Grant.

This book is divided into four sections. The first discusses the president's wives who have served as **First Lady.** The second features those **Wives** who were not First Ladies. The third section highlights the women who served as **Hostesses,** but were not married to presidents. The last section is filled with comparative data.

ACKNOWLEDGEMENTS

Thanks go to Dr. Roger Bridges and staff at the Rutherford B. Hayes Presidential Center; the Buffalo and Erie County Historical Society; Angela G. Horton, Assistant to the Curator, The White House; the National Society of the Daughters of the American Revolution; "Mr. First Lady"—Dr. Walter A. Ostromecki, Jr.; Dr. Clifford A. Pease, Jr.; The Smithsonian Institution; Fred L. Worth. Assistance with medical terminology was provided by Michael J. Paletta, M.D. Proofreading was performed by Ellen Perry Collier and editorial assistance given by LMP.

FIRST LADIES

MARTHA DANDRIDGE CUSTIS WASHINGTON

(1731–1802)
First Lady 1789–1797

The Straight Facts

Born: June 21, 1731
Birthplace: New Kent County, Virginia
Ancestry: English
Physical Characteristics: 5′ tall, brown hair, hazel eyes
Religion: Episcopalian
Husbands: Daniel Parke Custis (1711–1757)
    George Washington (1732–1799)
Date of Marriages: (1) June 6, 1749
     (2) January 6, 1759
Place of Marriages: (1) New Kent County, Virginia
      (2) New Kent County, Virginia
Children: (1) Two sons, two daughters
    (2) None

Died: May 22, 1802
Place of Death: Mount Vernon, Virginia
Burial Place: Mount Vernon, Virginia
Firsts: To be born in Virginia
      To own slaves
      Widow to marry a future president
      To serve as First Lady in her fifties
      To be older than her husband
White House Portrait: Eliphalet F. Andrews, East Room

The More Colorful Facts

Astrological Sign: Cancer
Nicknames: Patsy, Lady Washington, Mother of our Country
Childhood and Family Life: Martha, the oldest of eight children of Colonel John Dandridge and Frances Jones, was born at their Chestnut Grove plantation in Virginia. The athletic Martha was educated at home but preferred riding horses to reading. This is borne out by her few surviving letters which show her to be a poor speller and grammarian whose handwriting is almost illegible. She was taught by her mother how to run a plantation and was schooled in the "wifely arts" of knitting, sewing, weaving, dancing, menu planning, food preservation, making medicines, and childrearing. She made her debut in Williamsburg society at age fifteen.
First Husband: At eighteen she married her godfather, Daniel Parke Custis, who was twenty years her senior, at St. Peter's (then known as the Brick Church) in New Kent County, Virginia by the Rev. David Mossum. The couple lived at Custis's estate, which was called the White House, near Williamsburg. Family decree mandated that any offspring born to the couple must have "Parke" as a middle name or forfeit his or her inheritance. It was a happy marriage, lasting ten years until Custis died of a fever at forty-five years of age. Upon his death, Martha became one of the wealthiest landowners in Virginia, owning over 20,000 acres, two homes, 200 slaves, and nearly 23,000 British pounds sterling.
Courtship and Marriage: On March 16, 1758, while visiting Colonel and Mrs. Richard Chamberlayne at Poplar Grove, their estate on the Pamunkey River, the young widow was introduced to Col. George Washington. Washington's two-hour stopover turned into an overnight stay, as he was thoroughly captivated by Martha. Within ten days he visited Martha at her estate and proposed; eight months and only four meetings later they were married. The Rev. Mossum again officiated at the ceremony, held at Martha's estate. The twenty-six-year-old groom wore the dress blue uniform of his regiment, The First Virginia. Lined with

red silk, it was worn over a white silk waistcoat adorned with gold buckles. A dress sword completed the outfit. Three bridesmaids attended the twenty-seven-year-old bride who wore a yellow silk dress with a lace neckline and adorned with pearls. The ring, ordered from Philadelphia, cost two pounds, sixteen shillings. After three days of celebration, the family went to live at Six Chimneys, Martha's estate in Williamsburg.

Children: The Washingtons had no children. By Daniel Custis, Martha had two sons and two daughters. Two—a son and a daughter—died of fever in infancy. Martha (Patsy) died in 1773 at sixteen of what was probably epilepsy. Only John Parke (Jacky) lived to adulthood. He died of camp fever during the Revolutionary War at age twenty-seven, leaving two children who were taken in by the Washingtons. Out of deference to the Custis family, Washington did not adopt Martha's children, but he raised them as his own and indulged them just as much as she did.

Personal Notes: Short, plump, and with an "agreeable face and air," Martha was also known for her temper. She was deeply religious and spent one hour each morning at devotions, leaving strict orders never to be disturbed. An accomplished horsewoman, her favorite mounts were Fatima, Graylegs, and Foxglove. She loved to dance and wore size five slippers. Unlike George Washington, she had strong white teeth and ground her own tooth powders. She played the harpsicord and spinet and could sing. Shortly after their wedding. Washington gave her a songbook specially ordered from England: *The Bull Finch. A Choice Collection of the Newest and Most Favorite English Songs which have been set to Music and Sung at the Public Theatres and Gardens.*

General's Wife: The Washingtons divided the first sixteen years of their married life between Six Chimneys and Mt. Vernon, Washington's family estate. When he assumed command of the Continental Army in 1775, Martha remained at Mt. Vernon, running the estate. British troops often threatened but never invaded the estate. She made seven trips to Colonial headquarters during the war and endured the hardships of Valley Forge. She tended the wounded, mended their clothes, and fed them from provisions brought from Mt. Vernon. She encouraged other wives to sew, spin, and weave clothes for the soldiers, telling them they must be "patterns of industry." Martha wore only American homespun and encouraged others to do the same. Most importantly, she supported her husband through the darkest days of the Revolution.

First Lady: Martha did not accompany her husband to New York for the first inauguration in 1789. The couple couldn't afford it—George had to borrow money to travel to New York. Martha stayed to close up Mt. Vernon and joined Washington in May 1789, traveling to New York in her yellow and white "Penn Coach," given to her by the people of Pennsylvania in gratitude for her efforts during the Revolutionary

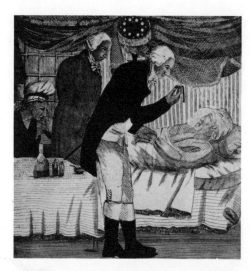

An early nineteenth-century print shows Washington dying attended by Martha and his physicians.

War. The first "presidential home" was that of Samuel Osgood at One Cherry Street. Martha was quite surprised at the interest and praise given "Lady Washington." Her only public speech as First Lady was a "thank you" at the reception given for her by New Yorkers. For Washington's second inauguration in 1793, her inaugural gown was russet colored with lace around the neck. She set new fashion trends by wearing a kerchief around her neck and a white mobcap for social occasions. As First Lady, she held receptions on Fridays between 7 and 9 P.M. The wife of the vice-president, Abigail Adams, was always seated at her right. The Washingtons moved to Philadelphia in 1790, when the nation's capital changed, residing at 190 High Street, the home of financier Robert Morris. Martha never lived in the White House or resided in Washington as First Lady.

Death: After Washington died in 1799, Martha burned all their letters to each other. She died one month shy of her seventy-first birthday of a severe fever, after seventeen days of illness. Knowing that the end was near, she picked out her own burial gown and received communion from her pastor. In her will, she freed all the slaves at Mt. Vernon. She had given Congress permission for George's (and her) remains to be buried beneath the new Capitol building in Washington, D.C. However, by the time the crypt was ready, her descendents refused permission, and George and Martha Washington lie in a vault at Mount Vernon.

ABIGAIL SMITH ADAMS

(1744–1818)

First Lady 1797–1801

The Straight Facts

Born: November 22, 1744
Birthplace: Weymouth, Massachusetts
Ancestry: English
Physical Characteristics: 5'1" tall, brown hair, brown eyes
Religion: Congregational
Husband: John Adams (1735–1826)
Date of Marriage: October 25, 1764
Place of Marriage: Weymouth, Massachusetts
Children: Three sons, two daughters
Died: October 28, 1818
Place of Death: Quincy, Massachusetts
Burial Place: First Parish Church, Quincy, Massachusetts

Firsts: To live in the White House
To cross the Atlantic
To be the mother of a president
To be the wife of an ambassador to the Court of St. James's
To be born in Massachusetts
Official Portrait: Ralph Earl or Mather Brown, New York State Historical Society

The More Colorful Facts

Astrological Sign: Sagittarius
Nicknames: Abby, Ardent Patriot, Mrs. Presidentress, Dear Partner, Miss Adorable, John's Helpmate
Childhood and Family Life: Abigail was the second child of William Smith and Elizabeth Quincy (pronounced Quin-zee). Her father was a third-generation Congregationalist minister. She was related to John Alden and Priscilla Mullens. A weak and sickly child, Abigail did not go to school but was taught at home. Her father believed education was just as important for women as for men and insisted his daughters learn more than the "wifely arts." Abigail spent her childhood at three different homes—the parsonage of her father, the home of her uncle Isaac, and that of her maternal grandparents. She was a prolific letter writer who signed her notes using the childhood pseudonym of "Diana."
Courtship and Marriage: At the age of fifteen, Abigail met young attorney John Adams, a third cousin on her mother's side, while on a visit to her grandparents' home. During a five-year courtship, they corresponded almost daily, and, because John was a lawyer, Abigail used the pseudonym "Portia" from Shakespeare's *The Merchant of Venice.* They were wed in the parlor of the Smith home. The twenty-year-old bride wore a white, wide-skirted challis dress embroidered with tiny ruby flowers. The bride's father performed the ceremony, but his approval of the marriage had been reluctant as the law was not then the most honorable profession. This is evidenced by his choice of sermons: Matthew 11:18; "For John came neither eating or drinking, and they say 'He is possessed.' " After the ceremony, the couple mounted a single white horse and rode to their new home, which was located at 141 Franklin Street, Quincy, Massachusetts.
Children: The Adamses had five children. Abigail, called Nabby (1765–1813), like her mother, married a distant cousin, William Smith. John Quincy (1767–1848) became the sixth president of the United States. Charles (1770–1800), married the sister of brother-in-law William

Smith. Thomas (1772–1832) was chief justice of the Massachusetts Supreme Court. Susannah (1766–1770) died after only two years of life.

Personal Notes: An avid reader, Abigail loved Shakespeare and Molière. She was articulate, charming, tactful, a good judge of character, and a brilliant conversationalist. She loved music and taught herself French. She was also terrified of thunderstorms.

Patriot of the Revolution: Adams became very involved with secessionist activities following the passage of the Stamp Act. In 1767, the family moved to Boston's Brattle Square area to a home called the White House. In 1775, Abigail and son John Quincy watched the Battle of Bunker Hill from a nearby hillside. She donated part of her spoon collection to the minutemen to be melted into bullets. She took in refugees, nursed the wounded, and predicted a full-scale war. When John went to Philadelphia as a delegate to the Continental Congress, the couple began what was to become routine in their lives: long periods of separation. Abigail resurrected her habit of writing letters and kept her "Dearest Friend" advised as to what was happening with their family and in Massachusetts. Many of her letters have been preserved and they show great insight into the current political situation; they have become classic records of the American Revolution, filled with deep insight and strong moral convictions. An early suffragette, she urged her husband to "remember the ladies" in the new government and its policies. When Adams went to London and Paris, it was many months before she heard from him. While her husband was away, she used the skills learned from her Uncle Isaac and managed the household, controlled the finances, and educated the children. She became quite adept at bartering and investing.

Ambassador's Wife: In 1784, she traveled on the SS *Active* to join her husband at his post as the first ambassador of the United States to the Court of St. James's. Abigail became the first American woman presented at court. While in London, she attended lectures and learned about court customs and protocol.

Second Lady: When John was elected vice-president in 1789, they moved to Philadelphia. Abigail helped Martha Washington establish protocol and customs for the ladies. At receptions, she was seated next to Martha and would often provide the First Lady with names and information on guests. As wife of the vice-president she gave weekly receptions and a formal dinner for cabinet members on Wednesdays. These affairs were usually for gentlemen only. She also assisted her husband by receiving and paying calls. When Adams was elected to a second term, she returned to Massachusetts. Adams is often quoted as saying the office of vice-president was "the most insignificent office ever created by man." Abigail felt the wife of the vice-president was even more so.

First Lady: The illness of her mother-in-law prevented Abigail from attending her husband's inauguration in 1797. She joined him a few months later and they lived in the Tuncliffe Hotel in Philadelphia. Taking her experiences from European courts, she made her receptions much more formal and lavish than they had been under Martha Washington's hand. Abigail was often criticized for receiving guests on a thronelike chair, a custom set by her predecessor. But unlike Martha Washington, she became involved with political discussions and voiced her opinions on legislative matters.

The Adamses were the first to live in the unfinished "President's Palace" in the new Federal City or "The City in the Wilderness," as Washington was dubbed. On the week-long journey to their new home, they got lost outside of Baltimore and had to ask directions many times. On the way, many of their own family heirlooms were either lost, stolen, or broken. Arriving on October 16, 1800, they found only six rooms completed, no staircase, and no conveniences. The building was very cold and damp; Abigail had to keep fires burning in the eleven fireplaces twenty-four hours a day to keep some warmth in the rooms. She hung her laundry in the East Room to dry because it was the largest and had two fireplaces. The first reception, held New Year's Day 1801, was a big success and hundreds turned out to see the president's home.

Death: After leaving the White House, the Adamses lived at Peacefield, their home in Massachusetts, surrounded by their assorted grandchildren and their dog, Juno. The press dubbed them "Darby and Joan" after a couple in an English ballad. Abigail was frequently ill and confined to bed for weeks at a time. She contracted erysipelas, known as St. Anthony's Fire, a severe inflammation of the skin. She died at age seventy-four of typhus fever which affected her biliary system (liver). She was buried at the First Parish Church, now called the First Unitarian Church, in Quincy, Massachusetts.

DOROTHEA (DOLLEY) TODD PAYNE MADISON

(1768–1849)

First Lady (1809–1817)

The Straight Facts

Born: May 20, 1768
Birthplace: Guilford County, North Carolina
Ancestry: Irish, English
Physical Characteristics: 5'7" tall, black hair, blue eyes
Religion: Quaker, later Episcopalian
Husbands: (1) John Todd (1764–1793)
　　　　　　(2) James Madison (1751–1836)
Date of Marriages: (1) January 7, 1790
　　　　　　　　　(2) September 15, 1794
Place of Marriages: (1) Philadelphia, Pennsylvania
　　　　　　　　　　(2) Jefferson County, Virginia

Children: (1) Two sons
        (2) None
Died: July 12, 1849
Place of Death: Washington, D.C.
Burial Place: Montpelier Estate, Orange, Virginia
Firsts: To witness husband's inauguration
      To be born in North Carolina
      To serve as First Lady in her forties
      To be awarded a place of honor in Congress
White House Portrait: Gilbert Stuart, Red Room

The More Colorful Facts

Astrological Sign: Taurus
Nicknames: Dolley, Queen Dolley, Queen of Parties, Velvet Glove, Lady
    Presidentress
Childhood and Family Life: Dorothea was the second of six children of Virginia Quaker John Todd and Mary Coles. She was nicknamed Dolley when a younger brother could not pronounce Dorothea. She was taught by a tutor with her brothers and for a while attended a Friends' School. From her mother, she learned the "wifely arts"; from her maternal grandmother, who was not a Quaker, she learned about fashions, food, and jewelry. Eight-year-old Dolley was heartbroken when a brooch Grandmother Coles gave her fell off a chain she wore under her clothes. When Dolley was seventeen, her father freed his slaves, sold the farm, and moved to Philadelphia. The family starch business failed and Mary Payne was forced to turn her home into a boarding house to support the family.
First Husband: After a three-year courtship, Dolley married Philadelphia lawyer John Todd at the Pine Street Meeting House. In Quaker tradition, there was no minister, and the twenty-six-year-old groom and twenty-one-year-old bride pledged themselves to each other before eighty witnesses. Eliza Collins and Anthony Morris were the attendents. The newlyweds lived on Chestnut Street and had two sons. A yellow fever epidemic in Philadelphia during the spring of 1793 claimed the lives of Todd, their youngest son Temple, and Todd's parents. Dolley could not attend the funerals as she, herself, was recuperating from yellow fever.
Courtship and Marriage: Among those living at the Payne boarding house was New York Senator Aaron Burr. It was he who introduced Dolley to "the great little (James) Madison." Despite the differences in their ages (he was forty-three, she was twenty-three), their religions (he was Epis-

copalian, she was Quaker), and their sizes (he was 5'4", she was 5'7"), he ironed his suit. Dolley didn't accept Madison until she was summoned to have tea with her distant cousin, First Lady Martha Washington. Martha told Dolley she and the president approved of the marriage. Less than five months after meeting Madison, Dolley married him at the Harewood estate of her sister Lucy, who had married Washington's nephew, George Steptoe Washington. She was attended by Lucy and four others; Francis Madison served as his brother's best man. The Rev. Alexander Balmaine, a Madison cousin by marriage, officiated. For marrying out of her faith, Dolley was shunned by the Quakers.

Children: Dolley had no children by Madison. She had two children by John Todd. Temple, mentioned above, lived only a few months. (John) Payne Todd (1792–1852), was a spendthrift who went through his fortune and strapped his widowed mother on many occasions. He died unmarried and penniless.

Personal Notes: Dolley has been described as beautiful, gay, charming, witty, clever, and very gracious. She enjoyed fine wines, macaroons, and ice cream. Her favorite colors were gold and red. She could speak passable French and owned a brown macaw. She created new fashion trends and completely shed her Quaker background. Dolley was also very partial to snuff.

Politician's Wife: Once freed from the bonds of her strict Quaker upbringing, Dolley became a popular hostess and social leader. Since President Thomas Jefferson and his vice-president Aaron Burr were both widowers, Jefferson asked Dolley to serve as a hostess when "ladies were to be present." His choice of Dolley was based on three factors: Jefferson had been a suitor of her mother; Dolley helped raise his daughters; and Madison had been named Jefferson's secretary of state. She also helped raise and clothe Jefferson's grandchildren, assisted in his philanthropic work, and helped raise funds for the Lewis and Clark expedition. Following Jefferson's direction, all dinners were to be less formal than those of his predecessor and of republican simplicity. Dolley did not get involved with political matters, but she did become embroiled in the "Merry" incident.

British minister Anthony Merry and his regal wife were offended when Jefferson escorted Dolley instead of Mrs. Merry into a White House dinner. An official protest was filed, but Jefferson refused to bow to the whims of the British. When the Madisons gave a dinner and Mrs. Merry again was not escorted by the host, a second protest was filed. Dolley decided to soothe the Merrys by throwing a special dinner in their honor, but on the appointed day, the guests of honor failed to show up. The feud lasted until Merry was recalled to London.

First Lady: In 1809, Dolley became the first First Lady to witness her husband's inauguration. She was also the first to throw an inaugural ball, which was held at Long's Hotel. Over 400 guests attended and saw the new president dance with his wife who was gowned in yellow velvet adorned with pearls and a Parisian turban with Bird of Paradise plumes. With her excellent memory for names and faces, plus her good listening ability, she was a great asset to Madison.

Dolley hired French steward Jean Pierre Sioussat as her master of ceremonies. She preferred serving only American foods at dinners and her Wednesday evening levees were heavily attended. She also became well known for her sense of fashion. Even though she was taller than her husband, Dolley preferred wearing high heels, low-cut bodices, and she adopted Turkish turbans for everyday use.

It was son Payne Todd who suggested to his mother that Washington children be entertained by rolling eggs Egyptian style. Dolley thought it would be splendid fun and instituted the Easter Egg Roll on the grounds of the Capitol. She also presided at the first wedding held in the White House when her widowed sister, Lucy Washington, married Supreme Court Associate Justice Thomas Todd of Kentucky. Todd was a distant cousin of Mary Todd Lincoln.

During the War of 1812, entertaining in the White House was curtailed but not eliminated. In August 1814, British troops landed in Maryland and were intent on capturing Washington, the White House, and the president. Madison urged Dolley to gather a few belongings and leave. Literally leaving her uneaten dinner at the table, Dolley and a few trusted servants prepared to leave the White House. Dolley saved some of her jewelry and clothing, some silver, Madison's papers, the original copy of the Declaration of Independence, and the Gilbert Stuart portrait of George Washington. The last was saved because of Dolley's total devotion to the Custis grandchildren. She and her maid Matilda escaped and remained in hiding for three days until the British withdrew from Washington. They returned to find a burned-out city and White House and Madison trying to rebuild his government. It was Dolley who persuaded Madison not to relocate the capital back to Philadelphia but to stay and rebuild Washington City, as it was then called. While the White House was being rebuilt, the Madisons lived in Colonel Tayloe's Octagon House.

Queen of Washington: After eight years in the White House, the Madisons returned to their Montpelier, Virginia, home. Dolley continued to entertain, and the couple's home was just as filled with guests as if they had remained in Washington. As Madison's health declined, Dolley became his nurse and read to him constantly. She also took dictation from him and helped organize his papers. Upon Madison's death, she

A trendsetter in fashion, Dolley Madison adopted the Turkish turban for everyday use.

moved back to Washington. She continued to entertain lavishly, attend parties, and support philanthropic causes. It was said that while other ladies would give away pints of milk to starving children, Dolley would give the whole cow. She was also constantly strapped for funds as son Payne went through both of their fortunes. She was forced to sell her spoons, her husband's papers and books, and even her home to pay off her son's debts. Fur merchant John Jacob Astor bought the mortgage on her house at 16th and H Street and allowed her to live there nearly rent free.

Even into her seventies and eighties, Dolley was the grand dame of Washington and knew the next eight presidents. She participated in the ceremonies for the building of the Washington Monument. She arranged the marriage of cousin Angelica Singleton to one of Martin Van Buren's sons, and attended the test firing of the Peacemaker cannon in which six people were killed. Congress awarded her high honors by bestowing franking privileges on her and voting her a lifelong seat on the floor of the House.

Death: By the time Dolley died at the age of eighty-one, she had been the queen of Washington society for over fifty years. Her funeral attracted the largest crowd that ever attended services at St. John's Episcopal Church. She was first buried in Congressional Cemetery but was later moved to Montpelier, where her husband had been buried.

ELIZABETH KORTRIGHT MONROE

(1768–1830)

First Lady (1817–1825)

The Straight Facts

Born: June 30, 1768
Birthplace: New York, New York
Ancestry: Dutch, English
Physical Characteristics: 5'4" tall, black hair, blue eyes
Religion: Episcopalian
Husband: James Monroe (1758–1831)
Date of Marriage: February 16, 1786
Place of Marriage: New York, New York
Children: One son, two daughters
Died: September 23, 1830
Place of Death: Oak Hill, Virginia

Burial Place: Hollywood Cemetery, Richmond, Virginia
Firsts: To be born in New York
   To have a daughter marry in White House
White House Portrait: Unknown artist, Blue Room

The More Colorful Facts

Astrological Sign: Cancer
Nicknames: La Belle Americaine, Belle of New York, Eliza
Childhood and Family Life: Elizabeth was the priviliged daughter of Captain Laurence Kortright, a founder of the New York Chamber of Commerce, and Hannah Aspinwall. There were four other children, and the four girls were all educated at home.
Courtship and Marriage: The Kortrights were leaders of New York society. Elizabeth and her sisters all had debuts and Elizabeth was the darling of the society set. She and her sisters traveled extensively in Europe. At one social function, Elizabeth met the delegate to the Continental Congress from Virginia, James Monroe. She quickly captured his eye and their courtship consisted of gay parties, dancing, and poetry readings. Her family did not approve of Monroe because he was not of the same social circle. Despite family reservations, Monroe and his "Smiling, Little Venus" were married at New York's Trinity Episcopal Church shortly before Elizabeth's eighteenth birthday. The couple honeymooned on Long Island.
Children: The Monroes had two daughters, and a son who lived only two years. The two girls assisted their mother in running the White House. Eldest daughter Eliza (1786–1835) married lawyer George Hay in 1808. His major claim to fame was as the prosecutor of former Vice-President Aaron Burr for treason. Younger daughter Maria Hester (1803–1850) married distant cousin Samuel Gouvernor in the White House on March 9, 1820, the first for a president's daughter. Gouvernor would later serve as his father-in-law's secretary.
Personal Notes: Elizabeth was an intelligent, quiet, reticent person who some thought aloof. She was a painter and could speak fluent French. Elizabeth was tall and graceful and noted for her slender, graceful arms and shoulders even into her sixties.
Ambassador's Wife: She accompanied Monroe when he took up posts as ambassador to France, England, and Spain. She charmed and impressed host countries, but the greatest test occurred in 1795 in France, which was in the midst of revolution. Although it was unwise for Monroe to become involved in French politics, his twenty-seven-year-old wife went to Le Petit Force prison in the official United States coach

with the purpose of calling on the wife of a hero of the American revolution, Madame Lafayette. Adrienne de Noailles (1760–1807) second daughter of the Duke d'Ayen, was fourteen when she wed Marie Joseph Paul Yves Roch Gilbert du Motier, Marquis de Lafayette (1757–1834) in 1774. Caught in the purge of the Revolution, she watched her mother, grandmother, and sister arrested and led away to the guillotine. Then she and her children were arrested. A tearful meeting was held in prison with the ambassador's wife. The French were impressed with Elizabeth's brave action and, as hoped, Adrienne and her children were released the next day. They left France using American passports under their surname, Motier, and joined the marquis in his Austrian prison of Olmutz until he, too, was released through American intervention two years later.

Politician's Wife: Upon their return from Europe, Elizabeth's health was not very good and they did little entertaining or visiting. The new secretary of state and his family were almost virtual unknowns to Washington society. Their home at 2017 I Street was not a regular stop on the social circuit.

First Lady: When Monroe was elected president in 1817, Elizabeth was suffering from a bad case of rheumatism. Although an elegant hostess, she changed the rules of society to ones that did not sit well with the public. She desired privacy and set her own schedule, not following what the public wanted. Her receptions were very stiff and formal and she received guests sitting on a raised platform. The practice of calling on ladies and returning their calls was discontinued by the First Lady. Any calls received were accepted, however. These duties were usually delegated to daughter Eliza Hay. When daughter Maria was married, Washington society was again offended. Due to her mother's ill health, Eliza decided the affair should be "New York style," very private and very small, with no one outside family and close friends invited. Society decided to retaliate by refusing to attend receptions where this eldest daughter was the hostess. Elizabeth was also known for her fashion sense, but was criticized for using cosmetics. She was glad to leave the White House after eight years.

Death: Living in cold, damp London while Monroe was ambassador to the Court of St. James's had contributed to Elizabeth's catching a rheumatic fever (inflammation of the heart valves and pain in the joints and muscles). The disease worsened in her later years, and she was beset by a series of violent seizures. She once fell into the fireplace at their Virginia estate, Ash Lawn, and was badly burned. She died of complications from the disease at age sixty-two. Monroe was so distraught at her death that he burned all of their letters to each other. Elizabeth is buried in Hollywood Cemetery near Richmond, Virginia

LOUISA CATHERINE JOHNSON ADAMS

(1775–1852)

First Lady (1825–1829)

The Straight Facts

Born: February 12, 1775
Birthplace: London, England
Ancestry: English
Physical Characteristics: 5′6″ tall, light brown hair, brown eyes
Religion: Episcopalian
Husband: John Quincy Adams (1767–1848)
Date of Marriage: July 26, 1797
Place of Marriage: London, England

Children: Three sons, one daughter
Died: May 14, 1852
Place of Death: Washington, D.C.
Burial Place: First Parish Church, Quincy, Massachusetts
Firsts: To be born in a foreign country
To be married in a foreign country
To bear a child in a foreign country
To bear a child on the Fourth of July
To have a son marry in White House
White House Portrait: Gilbert Stuart, Green Room

The More Colorful Facts

Astrological Sign: Aquarius

Childhood and Family Life: The only First Lady of foreign birth, London-born Louisa was the second of nine children of Joshua Johnson of Maryland and his British wife, Catherine Nuth. Joshua's brother, Thomas, was governor of Maryland and a signer of the Declaration of Independence. Joshua was a tobacco importer who took his family to France during the American Revolution since Americans were not popular in England. The family returned to London in 1790 when Joshua was named the first American consul. Louisa grew up speaking French just as fluently as English.

Courtship and Marriage: Just when she met future husband John Quincy Adams, son of the second president, is uncertain. When Adams returned to Europe in 1794, he called on the American consul and became reacquainted with the teenaged Louisa. Three years later, after a four-month engagement, the thirty-year-old diplomat married his twenty-two-year-old bride at the Church of the Parish of All Hallows in Barking, England. Anglican minister Mr. Hewitt officiated. Adams told his bride he loved her ". . . but [sic] love my country more." His family was opposed to the match as they did not believe her father was trustworthy. This was borne out when Joshua Johnson left town without paying the dowry. Adams's family did come to accept her and it was a good marriage, filled, if not with love, with mutual admiration and respect.

Children: In the first thirteen years of marriage, Louisa was pregnant eleven times but only three of the children lived. Eldest son George Washington Adams (1801–1829) drowned under mysterious circumstances in Long Island Sound. John Adams II (1803–1834) served as private secretary to his father, the president, and is the only presidential son to have married in the White House. Youngest son Charles Francis

(1807–1886) was a respected statesman and, in 1848, was the Free Soil party candidate for vice president. Their only daughter died an infant. Louisa took great pains to point out to her wayward teenage sons that she had come to her marriage a virgin.

Personal Notes: Louisa was an accomplished artist and musician. She played the harp and spinet and sang well. One of the most scholarly First Ladies, she was fluent in French and Greek, translated the classics, and wrote poetry. In 1826, she wrote a play called *Suspicion*. She also kept silkworms who ate mulberry leaves and spun silk used to make her dresses.

Ambassador's Wife: Due to her father's position, Louisa was well informed on protocol and court life. In Washington and abroad she charmed those around her and made up for her gruff husband. She once said he made a good guest but as a host lacked social charms. When Adams became minister to Russia in 1809, they left the oldest children with Abigail Adams, taking only little Charles, and sailed on the SS *Horace* on a stormy ten-week voyage. The Adamses endured many hardships during John Quincy's five years as minister, including the harsh winters, inadequate living quarters, lack of funds, and the loss of an infant daughter. Louisa's greatest adventures took place when she and young Charles went to join Adams in France, where he had been appointed peace commissioner in hopes of ending the War of 1812. Mother and son set out in midwinter on a perilous 2,000-mile, forty-day journey across Europe, which was involved in the Napoleonic Wars. The servants deserted them, their money was stolen, and both became ill. Nearing Paris, their coach was surrounded by French soldiers who were suspicious of the Russian coach. Only when Louisa, in fluent French, began addressing them and shouting "Vive la France" and "Vive l'Napoleon," were they allowed to proceed.

Politician's Wife: As wife of the secretary of state in the Monroe Administration, Louisa held receptions every Tuesday night and gave elegant theatre parties. Perhaps her greatest party was for the returning hero of the Battle of New Orleans, General Andrew Jackson. Over 800 guests attended the ball at the Adamses' F Street home. A poem was published in the *National Intelligencer* called "All are gone to Mrs. Adams" about the smashing event.

First Lady: Following the lead of predecessor Elizabeth Monroe, Louisa did not make calls as First Lady and returned only a select few. She also continued the formal entertaining style of the Monroes, but, because of her European background, her parties were more lavish. Louisa encouraged dancing at her parties and would often be seen in her size 1½ slippers sweeping the floor in a waltz or reel with a minister or politician. She also broke custom by mingling with guests and going from group to group and not receiving them surrounded by cabinet wives. The wedding of their son and a birthday party for the Marquis de La-fayette were two highlights of Louisa's tenure as First Lady. The final party before leaving the White House was a gay affair and even the out-going president is said to have enjoyed himself.

Death: Three years after being defeated for reelection to the presidency, Adams returned to Washington as the representative from Massachu-setts. Louisa was happy to be back in her F Street home. Ill health pre-vented her from being as involved as she wished, but she continued to be active in the Washington social scene. Adams died in the Speaker's Room in 1848, after collapsing from a stroke on the House floor. Con-gressmen would not let Louisa in the room to be with him when he died as Congressional offices were not a place for women. She lived four more years and suffered a stroke in 1849, which partially paralyzed her left side. She died at age seventy-seven and is buried next to her hus-band and in-laws in Quincy, Massachusetts.

ANNA TUTHILL HARRISON

(1775–1864)
First Lady (1841)

The Straight Facts

Born: July 25, 1775
Birthplace: Morristown, New Jersey
Ancestry: English
Physical Characteristics: Brown hair, brown eyes
Religion: Presbyterian
Husband: William Henry Harrison (1773–1841)
Date of Marriage: November 25, 1795
Place of Marriage: North Bend, Ohio
Children: Six sons, four daughters

Died: February 25, 1864
Place of Death: North Bend, Ohio
Burial Place: William Henry Harrison State Park, North Bend, Ohio
Firsts: Not to assume any duties of First Lady
      To lose her husband to death in office
      To regularly attend school
      To receive a pension of $25,000
      To be born in New Jersey
      To elope
      To be the grandmother of a president
Official Portrait: Cornelia Stuart Cassady, Benjamin Harrison Home,
      Indianapolis, Indiana

The More Colorful Facts

Astrological Sign: Leo
Childhood and Family Life: Anna was the second daughter of Judge John
    Cleves Symmes, sometime chief judge of the New Jersey Supreme
    Court, and his first wife, Anna Tuthill. During the Revolutionary War,
    Judge Symmes disguised himself in a British uniform and smuggled his
    four-year-old motherless daughter to her grandparents in New York.
    She was raised there and attended a series of schools including Clinton
    Academy and Miss (Isabella) Graham's Boarding School. At nineteen,
    she joined her father and his second wife in Ohio, where he had been
    appointed a territorial judge/governor.
Courtship and Marriage: At an officer's reception at Fort Washington, Anna
    met Captain William Henry Harrison. They fell in love immediately,
    but Judge Symmes refused to give his consent. On a day when the judge
    was away on business, the two eloped, marrying in the home of the lo-
    cal justice of the peace, Dr. Stephen Wood. Incensed that his twenty-
    year-old daughter would marry against his wishes, the judge accosted
    the twenty-two-year-old groom and asked how he would support his
    daughter. "With my sword and good right arm!" was the reply. Only af-
    ter Harrison excelled as a military leader did Symmes accept his son-
    in-law.
Children: Anna had the most children of any First Lady. Of her ten chil-
    dren, she survived all but one. The survivor, John Scott, was the father
    of the twenty-third president, Benjamin Harrison, making her the only
    First Lady to be the grandmother of a president.
Personal Notes: Not much is known about her life. She was a good house-
    keeper, ran the estate well, could knit, sew, and play the piano.

Politician's Wife: Anna spent most of her life in North Bend, running the household and raising the children while Harrison was away. She did take one trip to Philadelphia when Harrison was first elected to Congress. She spent six months with him on the trip and enjoyed the parties and social whirl.

First Lady: She had the shortest tenure of any First Lady. Anna was suffering from influenza when the time came for her husband to leave for Washington. Forbidden to travel for three months, she sent widowed daughter-in-law Jane Irwin Harrison to set up housekeeping in the White House. Thirty-one days after taking the oath of office and delivering a 8,555-word inaugural address in the pouring rain wearing neither overcoat nor hat, Harrison died of pneumonia. One can only wonder what would have happened had she been there to supervise his wardrobe on the day of inauguration. She is the only First Lady not to assume any of her official duties.

Post White House: She spent most of the twenty-two years of her widowhood living quietly in North Bend. Congress awarded her Harrison's entire first year's salary of $25,000, the first pension ever paid to a First Lady; she was also awarded franking (free postage) privileges. Deeply religious, she was a firm supporter of her church. She lived alone until her home burned in 1855 and then moved in with a son and his family.

Death: Her health failed in later years and she died at eighty-eight in the home of her son, John Scott Harrison. The day of her funeral was one of mourning and nearly the entire town of North Bend turned out. They heard the Reverand Horace Bushnell eulogize her on the theme of "Be Still and Know I am God." She was buried next to her husband in North Bend.

LETITIA CHRISTIAN TYLER

(1790–1842)
First Lady (1841–1842)

The Straight Facts

Born: November 12, 1790
Birthplace: New Kent County, Virginia
Ancestry: English
Physical Characteristics: Brown hair, brown eyes, olive complexion
Religion: Episcopalian
Husband: John Tyler (1790–1862)
Date of Marriage: March 29, 1813
Place of Marriage: New Kent County, Virginia
Children: Three sons, five daughters

Died: September 10, 1842
Place of Death: Washington, D.C.
Burial Place: Cedar Grove Plantation, New Kent County, Virginia
Firsts: To be born an American citizen
To marry husband on his birthday
To die while her husband was in office
To die in the White House
Official Portrait: Unknown artist, private collection of John Tyler Griffin

The More Colorful Facts

Astrological Sign: Scorpio
Childhood and Family Life: Letitia was the third daughter of planter Robert
Christian and Mary Brown. She had six sisters and two brothers, and
they all grew up at Cedar Grove, the family plantation.
Courtship and Marriage: John Tyler met the dainty, shy Miss Christian at a
neighborhood party. He claimed it was love at first sight and that he
had to beat out numerous other suitors. They were engaged for five
years while Tyler set up his law practice. It wasn't until three months
before their March 29, 1813 wedding that he dared to kiss his twenty-
three-year-old fiancée and then it was on the hand. Following the ceremony, held at the Christian family estate, they lived at "Mons Sacer,"
part of the Tyler family's Greenwood estate.
Children: The Tylers had eight children. The three sons all served the Confederacy during the Civil War, as did a son-in-law and several grandsons. One of their grandsons married the niece of the Confederate First
Lady, Varina Davis, at the Richmond White House.
Personal Notes: Knitting was Letitia's favorite hobby, followed by gardening. Roses were her favorite flowers.
First Lady: Letitia suffered a stroke in 1839 and was not strong enough to
withstand the rigors of being First Lady. Most duties were assumed by
daughter-in-law Priscilla Cooper Tyler and, to a lesser degree, daughter
Letitia Tyler Semple. Confined to a wheelchair, her only public ap-
pearance during her tenure was the wedding of daughter Elizabeth
(Lizzie) to William Waller in 1842.
Death: Letitia succumbed to the effects of her stroke and died in the White
House at age fifty-two. Family legend says she died holding a damask
rose. She is buried at Cedar Grove.

JULIA GARDINER TYLER
(1820–1889)
First Lady (1844–1845)

The Straight Facts

Born: May 4, 1820
Birthplace: Gardiner's Island, New York
Ancestry: English
Physical Characteristics: 5'3" tall, black hair, gray eyes
Religion: Episcopalian, then Roman Catholic
Husband: John Tyler (1790–1862)
Date of Marriage: June 26, 1844
Place of Marriage: New York, New York
Children: Five sons, two daughters

Died: July 10, 1889
Place of Death: Richmond, Virginia
Burial Place: Hollywood Cemetery, Richmond, Virginia
Firsts: To be born in the nineteenth century
To be the subject of a newspaper interview
To marry a president while in office
To serve as First Lady in her twenties
To hire a press agent as First Lady
To have the child of a president after leaving the White House
White House Portrait: Francisco Anelli, East Wing Lobby

The More Colorful Facts

Astrological Sign: Taurus
Nickname: Rose of Long Island, Her Serene Loveliness
Childhood and Family Life: Julia was the oldest of three children of Senator
David Gardiner of New York and his fashionable wife, Juliana
McLachlen. She attend Chagaray Institute in New York City. She
made her debut at age fifteen, toured Europe, and posed for an ad for
New York department store Bogert and McCamly.
Courtship and Marriage: The Gardiner family were frequent guests at the
Tyler White House. Julia was introduced to President John Tyler by
Congressman Fernando Wood at a White House dinner. After the
death of his first wife, Tyler began to look romantically upon Julia. The
aggressor in the relationship, he proposed five times before she accepted; the first time was only six months after his first wife, Letitia, died.
On February 28, 1844, Tyler, Julia, and a host of other Washingto-
nians including Dolley Madison were among those who sailed on the
test run of the USS *Princeton,* the first propeller-driven warship. During the cruise, the ship's main gun, nicknamed the Peacemaker, mis-
fired and six people were killed, including Senator Gardiner. When Julia fainted at the news, the president himself carried her off the ship
and comforted her throughout her mourning. When she finally accepted his proposal of marriage, he was so overjoyed that he wrote a song in
her honor called "Sweet Lady Awake." He also imported an Italian
wolfhound named LaBeaux for her. The couple was married secretly
by the Right Rev. Benjamin Threadwell Onderdonk, Episcopal bishop
of New York, assisted by the Rev. Dr. Gregory Thurston Bedell. The
twenty-four-year-old bride wore a white dress with a gauze veil and a
circlet of flowers. Robert Tyler served as his fifty-four-year-old father's
best man at the ceremony held at New York City's Church of the As-
cension. The newlyweds took a honeymoon cruise on the Hudson and

spent their wedding night in a hotel room rented annually by Daniel Webster. Returning to Washington, they were given a wedding feast by Congress. John C. Calhoun helped cut the cake. Tyler's three sons from his first marriage accepted Julia, but his daughters did not.

Children: The Tylers had seven children. Two sons became doctors and one was the president of William and Mary College. Their last child was born when Tyler was over seventy years of age.

Personal Notes: Julia played the guitar and sang. She loved animals, especially birds and, even before meeting her husband, owned a canary named Johnny Ty. Raised an Episcopalian, she converted to Roman Catholicism twenty-seven years after leaving the White House. As a debutante, she created a fashion craze by wearing a diamond star on her forehead held in place with a gold chain. When her father died, she substituted a black stone for the diamond, which she called her Feronia.

First Lady: A fashionable First Lady, Julia received guests sitting on a platform flanked by young girls all dressed in white. She adapted the presidential anthem, 'Hail to the Chief," usually played by the Marine Corps band, from *The Knights of Snowden* by John Sanderson. The words were by Sir Walter Scott from *"The Lady of the Lake,"* Canto II. Julia served as First Lady for less than eight months. After Tyler's presidency, they returned to his Virginia retirement estate, Sherwood Forest, on the steamer SS *Curtis Peck.*

Politician's Wife: A Virginian by birth, Tyler sided with the southern cause. He headed an unsuccessful Washington peace conference in hopes of preventing war and later was elected to the Confederate Congress. Julia had a dream he was dying and rushed to Richmond to be with him. When she arrived, she found him in good health and he teased her for her impulse. The next day, he came into their room coatless, clutching his collar and tie, just as she had seen in her dream, and died a few days later. During the war, she served as a volunteer for the Confederacy. When federal troops invaded the Tyler estate in 1862, she took her children and fled to the Gardiner family home in New York.

Post White House: After the war, Julia divided her time between New York and rebuilding Sherwood Forest. In the wake of the Garfield assassination, all presidents' widows were given pensions and she received $5,000 a year. In 1887, she granted an interview to famed reporter Nelly Bly.

Death: She died of a fever at age seventy-nine at the Richmond Hotel in room 27, directly across the hall from where her husband had died over a quarter of a century earlier.

SARAH CHILDRESS POLK

(1803–1891)

First Lady (1845–1849)

The Straight Facts

Born: September 4, 1803
Birthplace: Rutherford County, Tennessee
Ancestry: Scots-Irish
Physical Characteristics: 5'7" tall, black hair, dark eyes
Religion: Presbyterian
Husband: James Knox Polk (1795–1849)
Date of Marriage: January 1, 1824
Place of Marriage: Murfreesboro, Tennessee
Children: None
Died: August 14, 1891

Place of Death: Nashville, Tennessee
Burial Place: State Capitol grounds, Nashville, Tennessee
Firsts: To be born in Tennessee
      To act as secretary for her husband
      To be politically minded
White House Portrait: George Drury, after George P. A. Healy,
    East Wing Reception Room

The More Colorful Facts

Astrological Sign: Virgo
Nicknames: Sally, Puritan from Tennessee, The President's Guardian
Childhood and Family Life: Sarah was the daughter of Captain Joel Childress and Elizabeth Whitsitt. Sarah and her sister were first taught at home by Samuel P. Black of Murfreesboro Academy who taught their brothers during the day. The girls then attended the private school of Mr. Abercrombie and received piano lessons from his daughter. Finally, they attended the fashionable Moravian Female Academy in Salem, North Carolina.
Courtship and Marriage: She met lawyer James Knox Polk in the then state capital of Murfreesboro. The couple was married by the Rev. Dr. Henderson in the Murfreesboro Presbyterian Church on New Year's Day 1824. Among the guests at the twenty-year-old bride and her twenty-eight-year-old groom's wedding were Senator and Mrs. Andrew Jackson. Following two weeks of parties, the couple honeymooned in a hunting lodge near Rogersville, Tennessee.
Children: The Polks had no children of their own. In her later years, Sarah took in a namesake niece to be a companion during her widowhood.
Personal Notes: She is usually described as cultured, well read, and beautiful, with coloring resembling Spanish beauties. Her dark hair was worn in corkscrew curls. She was an avid needleworker, particularly excelling at cross-stitch. An ardent Calvinist, Sarah was a devout Presbyterian.
Politician's Wife: The Polks were popular with prominent members of the Democratic party. Both in Washington and in Nashville, Sarah was known for her charming and gracious manner. She was very helpful to Polk in his political career and served as his private secretary through his term in Congress and the White House.
First Lady: Politically astute and hard working, Sarah was a very involved First Lady. Socially, she served with a grave dignity. During her time, alcohol, dancing, and cards were banned from the White House. The Polks did attend the inaugural ball, but dancing was suspended. After

the president and his lady, dressed in a blue velvet gown with a fringed cape, left, the merriment picked up again. She did away with the extravagance usually associated with Washington soirées and carefully guarded the purse strings. Despite the formal, strict receptions, Sarah was well thought of in all levels of Washington society. At her last Sunday of worship as First Lady at the First Presbyterian Church, located at 4½ Street, the minister declared a day of mourning.

Post White House: Polk decided to serve only one term as president. They retired to their home called "Polk Place" in downtown Nashville. Exhausted by nearly four years of continual work and recurring attacks of cholera, Polk died barely four months after leaving office. Sarah was a widow at forty-six and spent the next forty-two years devoted to preserving his memory and working for her church. Each year on New Year's Day, the state legislature and various fraternal groups would pay tribute to her at Polk Place. During the Civil War, Sarah refused to leave Polk Place, and it was an undeclared neutral ground. She received generals from both sides, with no condemnation attached.

Death: Three weeks shy of her eighty-eighth birthday, Sarah died at Polk Place. The entire nation mourned her passing. She is buried next to her husband in Nashville on the State Capital grounds.

MARGARET MACKALL SMITH TAYLOR

(1788–1852)

First Lady (1849–1850)

The Straight Facts

Born: September 21, 1788
Birthplace: Calvert County, Maryland
Ancestry: English
Physical Characteristics: Brown hair, brown eyes
Religion: Episcopalian
Husband: Zachary Taylor (1784–1850)
Date of Marriage: June 21, 1810

Place of Marriage: Louisville, Kentucky
Children: One son, five daughters
Died: August 18, 1852
Place of Death: Pascagoula, Mississippi
Burial Place: Zachary Taylor National Cemetery, Louisville, Kentucky
Firsts: To be born in Maryland
Official Portrait: None

The More Colorful Facts

Astrological Sign: Virgo
Nickname: Peggy
Childhood and Family Life: Margaret was the daughter of Walter Smith, a planter and veteran of the Revolutionary War, and Ann Mackall (pronounced May-kle). Very little is known about her life; she had at least two brothers and one sister. Her mother died while she was in her teens and Margaret took over the running of the household. She had no formal education and was probably taught at home.
Courtship and Marriage: Two stories exist as to how Margaret met future husband Zachary Taylor. The most accepted says they were introduced by family friend Dr. Alexander Duke in 1809. Family legend says that they met when she was fourteen and he was a seventeen-year-old youth on the way to seek a commission in the army. Taylor and a friend sought shelter at the Smith home and Taylor was quite taken with the young girl. Six years later, he sought her out and they fell in love. They were married at the home of her sister, Mrs. Mary Chew, near Harrod Creek Station (Louisville). The bride was twenty-one and the groom twenty-five.
Children: Three daughters died of malarial fevers. Two died within a few months of each other in 1820, supposedly caused by the gaseous vapors associated with the bayous of Louisiana. Second daughter Sarah Knox eloped with an adjunct to her father, Lt. Jefferson Davis, in 1835, and died four months later. It would be years before Taylor forgave Davis for taking away his daughter. The remaining two daughters also married military men, who distinguished themselves during the Civil War on the Union side. Their only son, Richard, also served with distinction during the war, as a Confederate general.
Personal Notes: No authentic known picture of Margaret exists today. She was well read, smoked a pipe, and was very religious. For many years, she gladly followed her soldier husband around from post to post. Once the children were out of infancy, she sent them to relatives because she felt the frontier was no place for them. The family finally settled in

Louisville. She was a lifelong member of the American Sunday School Union.

First Lady: Taylor was apolitical and did not vote in any election, including his own. At first, he refused the Whig invitation to run as president, but he later consented. Margaret was not in favor of his running and prayed that opponent Lewis Cass would win. After Taylor returned safely from the Mexican War, Margaret vowed never to go into society again, and she never did. A reluctant First Lady, she spent most of her time secluded in her room on the second floor of the White House, which was decorated identically to her room in Baton Rouge. She also kept a sitting room at the top of the stairs. Frail, but not always weak, she preferred not to become involved. Most official duties were performed by youngest daughter Mary Elizabeth (Betty) Bliss or the second wife of former son-in-law Jefferson Davis, Varina Howell Davis. Margaret had a premonition that the presidency would be the death of her husband and it was. After Taylor died, she ordered no state funeral, no embalming, and left the White House immediately for a private burial in Louisville, Kentucky.

Death: She spent her remaining years quietly surrounded by her children and grandchildren. She also continued to teach Sunday school. She died at sixty-four of a fever in Mississippi and was buried next to her husband in Louisville. The Taylors are the first presidential couple to both die before a husband's four-year elected term was up.

ABIGAIL POWERS FILLMORE
(1798–1853)
First Lady 1850–1853

The Straight Facts

Born: March 13, 1798
Birthplace: Stillwater, New York
Ancestry: English
Physical Characteristics: 5'4" tall, red hair, blue eyes, fair skin
Religion: Unitarian
Husband: Millard Fillmore (1800–1874)
Date of Marriage: February 5, 1826
Place of Marriage: Moravia, New York
Children: One son, one daughter
Died: March 30, 1853
Place of Death: Washington, D.C.
Burial Place: Forest Lawn Cemetary, Buffalo, New York
Firsts: To work before and after marriage
To install a White House library
To install a bathtub and benefit from indoor toilets at the White House
Official Portrait: Unknown artist, Buffalo and Erie County Historical Society, Buffalo, New York

The More Colorful Facts

Astrological Sign: Pisces

Nickname: Abby

Childhood and Family Life: Abigail was the only daughter of Lemual Powers, a Baptist minister, and Abigail Newland. Upon her husband's death, Mrs. Powers took Abigail and her younger brother to Cayuga County, New York, in the belief that she could make her limited funds stretch more in the country. At the age of sixteen, young Abigail began teaching school in the summer to pay for her tuition for the winter.

Courtship and Marriage: Abigail met Fillmore when he began to attend classes she taught in Cayuga County. Although Fillmore would become a schoolteacher himself, he claimed she was the only schoolteacher he ever took lessons from. The couple was engaged for five years while Fillmore completed his studies and became a lawyer. They married at the home of her brother, with the Rev. Orasmus H. Smith of the Episcopal Church officiating. The bride was twenty-eight and the groom was twenty-six.

Children: The Fillmores had two children. Mary Abigail (1832–1854) often served as official White House hostess. She died of cholera one year after her mother. Millard Powers Fillmore (1828–1889) was a lawyer.

Personal Notes: Abigail could play the piano and harp, taught herself French, and was noted in Buffalo for her flower garden.

First Lady: By the time Fillmore became president, upon the death of President Zachary Taylor in 1850, Abigail was an invalid. Among other ailments, she had a weak knee which prohibited her from standing for long periods. Most official duties were taken over by her daughter, Mary Abigail. Neither Abigail nor Millard paid or received calls. Appalled by the lack of books in the White House, Abigail appropriated $250 from Congress to establish the first White House library. Deeply religious, she closed the executive mansion on Sundays so the family could meditate and pray. (Although Abigail's father was a Baptist minister, she was married by an Episcopal priest and later joined the Unitarian church.)

Death: She caught a cold after attending the inauguration of Franklin Pierce, who succeeded her husband as president. As no arrangements were made for her, she stood in the rain during the ceremony. William Makepeace Thackeray and Washington Irving stood with her. Abigail's cold developed into pneumonia and she died less than three weeks later at the age of fifty-five at the Willard Hotel in Washington, D.C.

JANE MEANS APPLETON PIERCE

(1806-1863)
First Lady 1853-1857

The Straight Facts

Born: March 12, 1806
Birthplace: Hampton, New Hampshire
Ancestry: English
Physical Characteristics: 5'5" tall, 90 lbs., brown hair, brown eyes
Religion: Congregationalist
Husband: Franklin Pierce (1804-1869)
Date of Marriage: November 19, 1834
Place of Marriage: Amherst, New Hampshire
Children: Three sons
Died: December 2, 1863
Place of Death: Andover, Massachusetts

Burial Place: Old North Cemetery, Concord, New Hampshire
Firsts: To be born in New Hampshire
To install a furnace in the White House
Official Portrait: Unknown daguerreotype, Pierce Brigade House, Concord, New Hampshire

The More Colorful Facts

Astrological Sign: Pisces
Nickname: Jeanie, Reluctant First Lady, Shadow in the White House
Childhood and Family Life: Jane had a strict religious upbringing as the daughter of Bowdoin College president Rev. Jesse Appleton and Elizabeth Means. She was well educated for a woman of the times but suffered from frail health. Her father did not believe in fresh air or physical activity for girls.
Courtship and Marriage: She met Franklin Pierce while he was a student at Bowdoin. Neither she nor her family encouraged the courtship. She, because of her religious feelings, and her family, because Pierce was not of the same social class. After a six-year engagement while Pierce was establishing his law practice, they were married. The twenty-eight-year-old bride, dressed in traveling clothes and a bonnet, was escorted down the aisle by her brother, Robert Appleton. Brother-in-law Rev. Silas Aiken performed the ceremony at his own home, and after a brief reception, the newlyweds left for Washington.
Children: The Pierces had three sons, none of whom lived to adulthood. Franklin, Jr. lived only a few days. Frank Robert died of typhus at age 4. Benjamin (Bennie) died tragically at age eleven. On January 6, 1853, the family boarded a train to attend the funeral of family friend Amos Lawrence. The train derailed and the only passenger to be killed was Bennie, who was crushed before his parents' eyes. Neither parent really ever recovered from the tragedy.
Personal Life: Jane was slender, shy, and melancholy. She had chestnut hair, which was usually worn parted in the middle with two corkscrew curls on each side. Deeply religious, she advocated temperance. She spent much of her time visiting relatives, separated from her husband because she believed a northern climate was better for her consumption (tuberculosis) than hot, humid Washington.
Politician's Wife: The newlywed congressman and his wife began their married life at Birth's Boarding House for ten dollars a week and one dollar and fifty cents per session for the use of a rocking chair. Religious Jane did not take to the lavish nightly entertainment in Washington and spent most of the time in her room. She persuaded Pierce to give up

politics in 1842 and they returned to Concord, New Hampshire. He declined other appointments including a cabinet position, in deference to her. Jane thought he had left public office for good until he accepted the nomination for president. When she heard the news, she fainted.

First Lady: Jane lived in Baltimore for the first six months of her tenure because she couldn't stand the thought of living in the White House. Bennie had died two months before the inauguration and she believed it was God's way of punishing them for leaving home. When she finally did move into the White House, she spent most of the time in her bedroom writing letters to Bennie. Most formal entertaining was left to her aunt Abby Kent Means or the wife of the secretary of war, Mrs. Jefferson Davis (the former Varina Howell). In the last year of Pierce's presidency, she did host a few events which were very strict and formal.

Post White House: Upon leaving the White House in 1857, the Pierces sailed to Europe on the SS *Powhatan*, a government ship loaned to them by President James Buchanan. They spent over three years visiting Portugal, Spain, France, Switzerland, Italy, Belgium, Austria, and England.

Death: Jane's melancholy increased in later years as her health failed. She died at age fifty-seven of tuberculosis in Andover, Massachusetts. Pierce brought her home to rest with their sons at Old North Cemetery in Concord, New Hampshire.

MARY ANN TODD LINCOLN

(1818–1882)
First Lady 1861–1865

The Straight Facts

Born: December 13, 1818
Birthplace: Lexington, Kentucky
Ancestry: Scots-Irish
Physical Characteristics: 5'1" tall, 95 lbs., light brown hair, blue eyes
Religion: Episcopalian
Husband: Abraham Lincoln (1809–1865)
Date of Marriage: November 4, 1842
Place of Marriage: Springfield, Illinois
Children: Four sons
Died: July 16, 1882
Place of Death: Springfield, Illinois

Burial Place: Oak Ridge Cemetery, Springfield, Illinois
Firsts: To be born in Kentucky
To lose a husband by assassination
To be committed to an asylum
White House Portrait: Katherine Helm, Lincoln Bedroom

The Colorful Facts

Astrological Sign: Sagittarius
Nicknames: Molly, She-Wolf, Queen, Presidentress, Little Sister, Mother, Puss, Hell-Cat
Childhood and Family Life: Mary Ann Todd was the third daughter and fifth child of banker Robert Smith Todd and his first wife, Eliza Ann Parker. Eliza died when Mary was seven and, sixteen months later, Todd married Elizabeth (Betsey) Humphreys, by whom he had nine additional children. A vibrant, athletic girl, Mary attended Dr. John Ward's Seminary in Lexington until she was fourteen, when she and a sister were sent to a boarding school run by Madame Victoria Charlotte LeClere Montelle, late of the French court.
Courtship and Marriage: Upon graduation, Mary went to live with her sister, Elizabeth (Mrs. Ninian Wirt Edwards), in Springfield, Illinois. At a cotillion, she was introduced by lawyer Joshua Speed to fellow lawyer Abraham Lincoln. Lincoln told her he wanted "to dance with her in the worst way" and, she told friends, he did. After a stormy courtship, the couple became engaged. Mary chose Lincoln over others, including Stephen Douglass, "because he had the best chance of becoming President of the United States." The wedding was set for early 1841. For undisclosed reasons, the engagement was broken off; some have even said the bride was left at the altar to face the guests alone. Lincoln was suffering from a deep depression during that time and friends despaired for his life. In late 1842, the couple became engaged again, and the wedding was set for November 4. On a rainy night, the twenty-three-year-old bride met the thirty-three-year-old groom in the parlor of the Edwards home. She wore her sister Frances's white satin gown with a strand of pearls. Attendants were Miss Julia Jayne (later Mrs. Lyman Trumbull), cousin Miss Eliza Todd, and a Miss Rodney. The best man was James H. Manthey, and the ceremony was performed by Dr. Charles Dresser. The ring's inscription read "To M.T. from A.L. Love Is Eternal, Nov. 4, 1842." After a brief honeymoon to meet the bride's family in Lexington, the Lincolns returned to Springfield, where they took up residence in the Globe Tavern for four dollars per week. It was a stormy marriage but Mary did come to love Lincoln and if there was

not love on his part, there was great affection. The marriage lasted nearly twenty-three years.

Children: The Lincolns had four sons and only the oldest lived to adulthood. Robert Todd (1843–1926) was a lawyer, businessman, and politician who married Mary Eunice Harlan (1846–1937) in 1868. They had two children. Robert believed himself a jinx because he was personally, politically, and geographically close to the first three assassinated presidents. After McKinley's death, he vowed never to appear in public again with a president and kept that vow for the final twenty-five years of his life. The youngest sons all died of fevers. Edward Baker died at age four before the family left Springfield; William Wallace died at age twelve in the White House; and Thomas (Tad) died at eighteen, shortly after returning from Europe with his mother. Tad had a misshapen palate and lisped; he was indulged by both parents and was a terror in the White House. After being made an honorary lieutenant in the army, he drilled troops and tried to fire a cannon from the White House roof.

Personal Notes: Mary was fluent in French, could sew, and loved the opera. She has been described as witty, articulate, gracious, vivacious, and flirtatious. She was well read and her favorite authors were Spenser, Whittier, Pope, Longfellow, and Elizabeth Barrett Browning. She liked bright-colored clothing and rooms and favored pink, lavender, magenta, yellow, and bright blue. She was known for her stylish fashions, preferring décolletage dresses and flowers in her hair.

First Lady: Destined to be the most maligned First Lady of all time, Mary's entrance into Washington was nearly as tragic as her leaving. In both cases, she was without her husband and there were no crowds to cheer her. When Lincoln was elected to the presidency, Mary was elated, as her vow to marry a man who would become president had come true. She made plans for closing up their house, bought a new wardrobe, and dreamed of the lavish parties she would throw. In what is known as the "Baltimore Plot," aides (and Mary) feared Lincoln would be assassinated by secessionists before entering Washington. Lincoln was forced to don a disguise and leave the train before it entered the Baltimore-Washington train station. Mary and the children alone entered on the presidential train.

Mary found that neither the White House nor the position of First Lady was what she had envisioned. The War Between the States (as it was then called) curtailed her plans to become the social queen of Washington. However, she had several rooms in the White House redone, especially her favorite, the Red Room. She purchased a 700-piece set of Dorflinger crystal and a complete set of Haviland china.

Although Mary was unwavering in her loyalty to the Union, she was accused of treason and of being a Southern sympathizer. She compounded the rumors by inviting her widowed sister, whose husband died fighting for the Confederacy, to live in the White House. Unannounced, Lincoln appeared before a Senate committee testifying to her loyalty. It was well known but little reported in official Washington that Mary often visited hospitals, bringing food and clothing to the injured, writing letters to their families, and amusing them with tales of Lincoln and their family. She was just as good a mimic and storyteller as her husband.

The war ended one month after Lincoln's second inauguration. Mary looked forward to entertaining in the style she had envisioned five years earlier. Her dream was cut short, however, when her husband was shot before her eyes at Ford's Theatre.

Asylum: Mary was in deep mourning for son Willie for more than three years. She couldn't bear to look at his picture, the bedroom where he died, or the Green Room where he was embalmed. Her health failed; she suffered from obstetrical problems and terrible headaches. At one point, Lincoln threated to send her to "that large white building on the hill yonder," the government hospital for the insane. Her behavior became bizarre; she suffered from wide mood swings and deep periods of depression. At times, her spirits were bolstered by mediums because she believed in the hereafter.

Mary became obsessed with spending and acquiring goods. She ordered clothes, linens, perfumes, and household goods in large quantities. Dressmaker Elizabeth Keckley, whom she inherited when Varina Howell Davis (First Lady of the Confederacy) left Washington, was constantly making, altering, and changing the clothes Mary bought. She once ordered 3,000 pair of gloves, because she worried about losing one. During Lincoln's lifetime, he often paid off her debts and stopped her from trading political favors for jewels or clothes. At the time of Lincoln's death, she owed over $27,000 to various creditors.

When Lincoln was killed, the government awarded Mary a pension and the balance of his salary for the year, but she became obsessed with poverty, money, and death. In what was called the Old Clothes Scandal of 1867, Mary attempted to sell clothes to New York merchants before being stopped by son Robert. In 1868, she and Tad fled to Europe to escape creditors. While there, she sent a barrage of letters to Congress begging for more money. They returned in 1871, and Tad died shortly thereafter. The death of her husband and three of children was almost too much for Mary to bear.

She spent 1872 in Waukesha, Wisconsin, visiting the healing waters and consulting spiritualists. She traveled to Canada in 1873 and to Florida in 1874. While in Florida, she had a premonition of Robert's death and wired him and family friends that she was coming home to save him. Robert was in good health but had a hard time convincing his mother of this. Meanwhile, Mary continued to hoard and spend.

In 1875, Mary and Robert were living at the Grand Pacific Hotel in Chicago. She had caused Robert to become estranged from his wife. Mary would often knock on his door and tell wild stories of robbers and murderers. She continued to spend, and when she showed him the nearly $60,000 in cash she was carrying in her corset, he decided she needed help. A nurse was hired to stay with her, a bodyguard watched over her, and the law firm of Ayer & Kales decided her fate. It was determined that she was probably insane and could not take care of herself or her money. Robert petitioned the court to have her committed to an asylum and to have himself named executor of her estate. At the time, Illinois law stated that married women and infants who, in the judgement of medical professionals, were suspected as insane or deranged might be detained in the hospital at the request of the husband or a male relative with evidence of insanity. An insanity verdict was reached on May 19, 1875, and it was decided Mary would be sent to Bellevue Place in Batavia, Illinois. That evening, Mary twice attempted suicide by drinking a mixture of what she thought was laudanum and camphor. A wise druggist had filled her order with burnt sugar instead.

Bellevue Place was run by Dr. Robert Patterson. Located forty miles from Chicago, it catered to the upper crust of society and could accomodate thirty female patients. Mary had two rooms, a private nurse, and Robert took the ninety-minute train trip weekly to visit. Mary greeted him as a stranger and wrote numerous letters trying to attain her release. Among those receiving a letter was Myra Bardwell, the first female lawyer in Illinois.

Mrs. Bardwell visited Mary at Bellevue Place, thought her to be sane, and believed she was being held against her will. They appealed and, in September 1875, Mary was released to the custody of her sister, Elizabeth Edwards, but was still under a judgement of insanity. In June 1876, Myra got the verdict overturned, Robert removed as executor, and Mary was free.

Death: After the second trial, Mary went to France on the SS *Labrador* with sister Lizzie's grandson Edward Lewis Baker, Jr. Suffering from cataracts and arthritis, she was in poor health. She had two serious falls and decided to sail home on the *l'Amerique*. Another passenger on the ship was the noted actress, Sarah Bernhardt, who saved Mary from a fall on deck. When the ship docked in New York, the crowds that gathered greeted the Divine Sarah but ignored Mary. She returned to Springfield a broken woman. She often stayed in her room, lit by a single candle, staring into space. She died at sixty-four of a stroke and is buried next to her husband and sons in Oak Ridge Cemetery in Springfield.

ELIZA MCARDLE JOHNSON

(1810–1876)

First Lady (1865–1869)

The Straight Facts

Born: October 4, 1810
Birthplace: Leesburg, Kentucky
Ancestry: Scots-Irish, Welsh
Physical Characteristics: Brown hair, hazel eyes
Religion: Methodist
Husband: Andrew Johnson (1808–1875)
Date of Marriage: May 5, 1827
Place of Marriage: Greene County, Tennessee
Children: Three sons, two daughters
Died: January 15, 1876
Place of Death: Greeneville, Tennessee
Burial Place: Andrew Johnson National Cemetery, Greeneville, Tennessee

Firsts: To teach her husband to read and write.

To welcome a reigning monarch to the U.S.

Official Portrait: Byrd Venable Farioletti, after a photograph, The Smithsonian

The More Colorful Facts

Astrological Sign: Libra

Childhood and Family Life: Eliza was the only daughter of shoemaker/inn-keeper John McCardle (also seen as McArdle or McCardell) and Sarah Phillips. She attended Rhea Academy but was mostly educated at home where she helped her widowed mother run the family hostel.

Courtship and Marriage: Family legend says she met her future husband, Andrew Johnson, in 1826 when he and his widowed mother arrived in Greenville to set up a tailor shop. He asked directions of a group of girls and one made an unkind remark about the dirty, travel-weary group. Eliza supposedly rebuked her and said ". . . I like him and I'm going to marry him." She did marry him a year later at her mother's home when she was sixteen. The ceremony was performed by the local magistrate, Mordecai Lincoln, a distant cousin of the man who would have such an impact on their lives, Abraham Lincoln. It was a happy marriage and they were together for over forty-eight years.

Children: Two sons, Robert (1834–1869) and Charles (1830–1863), served the Union cause during the Civil War. The latter was killed when his horse fell on him. Youngest son, Andrew, Jr., (1852–1879) called Frank, was a newspaper publisher. Daughters Martha (1828–1901) and Mary (1832–1883) helped their mother by serving as official White House hostesses.

Personal Notes: Little is known of Eliza. She was pious and shy, could sew, knit, and was an avid reader. The latter hobby was important in her marriage because she taught her husband, who had been apprenticed to a tailor at age thirteen, how to read and write. After the birth of Frank in 1854, Eliza was diagnosed as having phthisis (slow consumption or tuberculosis) and became a semi-invalid.

Politician's Wife: Eliza was a gracious and charming, if reluctant, hostess while Johnson progressed through a series of political positions from alderman to mayor to state representative and governor. Her reluctance was based in part on the belief that she was inferior to city-bred, "society" ladies. She and Frank were forced to flee their home during the Civil War as Tennessee was a hostile state, half Union and half Confederate.

First Lady: It was a fearful, reluctant First Lady who entered the White House after the death of Lincoln. She had nightmares of Johnson also being assassinated. Most duties were performed by her daughters, especially Martha Patterson. She made only two formal appearances as First Lady; one at a reception for Queen Emma of the Sandwich Islands and one for children in honor of Johnson's sixtieth birthday. She preferred to stay in her small room in the northwest corner of the White House, reading her Bible and knitting. Johnson came calling each morning before going down to work. She had great faith in him and never believed he would be impeached.

Death: Eliza finally died of consumption (tuberculosis) in 1876, 168 days after her beloved husband. She was sixty-five and had been living at the home of her daughter, Mary. She is buried next to her husband in Greenville, as are all of their children.

JULIA BOGGS DENT GRANT
(1826-1902)
First Lady (1869-1877)

The Straight Facts

Born: January 26, 1826
Birthplace: St. Louis, Missouri
Ancestry: English
Physical Characteristics: Brown hair, brown eyes
Religion: Methodist
Husband: Ulysses Simpson Grant (1822-1885)
Date of Marriage: August 22, 1848
Place of Marriage: St. Louis, Missouri

Children: Three sons, one daughter
Died: December 14, 1902
Place of Death: Washington, D.C.
Burial Place: Grant's Tomb, Riverside Park, New York City
Firsts: To be born in Missouri
Official Portrait: Mathew Brady photograph, the Library of Congress

The More Colorful Facts

Astrological Sign: Aquarius
Nickname: Little Sister
Childhood and Family Life: Julia was the fifth of eight children of planter
  Col. Frederick Dent and Ellen Wrenshall. She was born at their home,
  White Haven. She was raised by her childhood nurse/slave, Black Kit-
  ty. Julia attended a local log schoolhouse until age ten, when she was
  sent to a boarding school run by the Misses Moreau.
Courtship and Marriage: Frederick Dent invited West Point classmate/
  roommate Ulysses S. Grant to visit the family home near St. Louis.
  Grant was smitten with the plain Miss Dent, drawn by her quick wit
  and charming ways. They took long rides together and read poetry.
  While crossing the swollen Mississippi, she asked if she could cling to
  his arm. He gave his assent and when they reached the other side, asked
  if she would like to cling to him for life. They were secretly engaged
  only three months after their first meeting, but, due to the length of the
  Mexican War, the engagement lasted over four years. It took Grant almost one year of that time to get the courage to ask the Colonel for his
  daughter's hand. At the wedding, the twenty-two-year-old bride wore a
  white gown from Paris of watered silk with lace. She was attended by
  Sarah Walker, sister Nellie Dent, and cousin Julia Boggs. The newly
  promoted captain was so nervous he kept getting his sword caught between his legs. The best man, James "Pete" Longstreet, and ushers
  Cadmus M. Wilcox and Bernard Pratt, would all serve in the Confederacy. The Rev. J. H. Linn officiated. Julia's father gave the Grants sixty
  acres of land and three slaves—Eliza, Dan, and Juliana. They took a
  four-month honeymoon, which included a prolonged visit to Grant's
  parents in Ohio. The elder Grants refused to attend the wedding because the Dents owned slaves. Grant called Julia "Mrs. G."; she called
  him "Ulys."
Children: The Grants had five children. Frederick Dent (1850–1912),
  named after his grandfather and uncle, like his father, went to West
  Point and became a general. He also served as police commissioner of
  New York City and ambassador to Austria-Hungary. Ulysses, Jr.

(1852–1929), known as Buck because he was born in Ohio, the Buckeye state, was a prominent lawyer in Republican affairs. Jesse Root (1858–1934) was a lawyer and wrote a book about his father. The only daughter, Ellen, known as Nellie (1855–1922), was born on the fourth of July and married Englishman Algernon Charles Frederick Sartoris at the White House in 1874. Both parents indulged and spoiled their children.

Personal Notes: Julia suffered from strabismus (crossed eyes), caused by a childhood boating accident. When it was suggested to Grant that she have the problem surgically corrected, he that he liked her that way. She was an excellent horsewoman whose favorite mounts were Psyche and Missouri Belle. She made many of her own clothes, was fond of Bret Harte novels, liked to draw, could dance, played the piano, and had a pleasant singing voice. She loved to garden and her favorite flowers were cape jessamines.

General's Wife: Whenever possible, Julia traveled with Grant from post to post, including stints in St. Louis, Detroit, and Sacketts Harbor, New York. She managed the household on his meager salary and tried to control his drinking. When Grant was transferred to the Pacific coast, she returned to White Haven, Missouri, where she bore their children. At the start of the Civil War, Grant was an unemployed tanner, barely scraping by as a farmer, at Hardscrabble, the family's home on the land Julia's father had given them. Rejected three times by the Illinois militia, he was finally accepted and given the rank of brevet colonel. The family moved to City Point to be near his headquarters. Julia helped tend the wounded, mend their uniforms, and boost morale. In 1862, she was nearly captured by Confederate troops near one of Grant's camps. In what is referred to as the *River Queen* incident, First Lady Mary Lincoln publically chastised Julia for sitting next to her on a couch without permission. Julia vowed to never appear again in public with the Lincolns. Three weeks later, when President Lincoln asked the Grants to go to the theatre, they declined, a decision they both would regret for the rest of their lives. After the war, the Grants were offered three homes in Washington. They chose one at 205 I Street in Washington and lived there during Grant's tenure as secretary of war (1867–1868).

First Lady: Gracious and well mannered, Julia enjoyed welcoming crowds to the White House. The Grants wanted to continue living at their I Street home and use the White House for official business. This idea was quickly rejected as the new president was hounded by job seekers. Every Tuesday afternoon Julia received guests, assisted by cabinet wives; orders were given that no one was to be turned away. Every Wednesday evening, lavish dinners for thirty-six were held, with up to

Julia (third from the left) was reluctant to go down when the Grants explored a mine in Virginia City, Nevada, in 1879, but quickly changed her mind when she heard Grant (center) had bet a dollar she was afraid.

twenty-nine courses. Italian steward Melah managed these affairs, which cost up to $2,000 per week. To obtain some privacy, the Grants bought a home in Long Branch, New Jersey, a resort area founded in 1778 for wealthy Philadelphians. Despite the "spoils scandals" of the Grant administration, socially they were favorites and quite popular.

Death: After leaving the White House, the Grants sailed the SS *Indiana* for a 2½ year tour of Europe, the Orient, and, much to Julia's delight, the Holy Land. They were the toast of the continent and were lauded by royalty at every stop. Returning to New York, Julia urged Grant to run for a third term in 1880; he said he would accept but not campaign for the nomination which went to James Garfield. Grant finished his memoirs just weeks prior to his death and Julia spent the rest of her life living off the royalties. She traveled, visited her family, attended a namesake granddaughter's wedding to a Russian prince, supported the suffrage movement, and attended Grand Army of the Republic events in honor of her husband. She found comfort in the friendship of Varina Howell Davis, widow of Confederate preisident Jefferson Davis, and with Susan B. Anthony and her suffragettes. In 1902, she became ill with bronchitis, compounded by kidney and heart disease. She died a few months later, at age seventy-six, and is buried next to her husband in Grant's Tomb. The Rev. Dr. Frank Bristol of the Metropolitan Methodist Church officiated at the funeral services.

LUCY WARE WEBB HAYES
(1831–1889)
First Lady (1877–1881)

The Straight Facts

Born: August 28, 1831
Birthplace: Chillicothe, Ohio
Ancestry: English
Physical Characteristics: 5'4" tall, 161 lbs. black hair, hazel eyes
Religion: Methodist
Husband: Rutherford Birchard Hayes (1822–1893)
Date of Marriage: December 30, 1852
Place of Marriage: Cincinnati, Ohio
Children: Seven sons, one daughter
Died: June 25, 1889

Place of Death: Fremont, Ohio
Burial Place: Rutherford B. Hayes Presidential Center, Fremont, Ohio
Firsts: To celebrate her 25th wedding anniversery in the White House
To be born in Ohio
To be the daughter of a doctor
To initiate the annual White House Easter Egg Roll
To be graduated from college
To visit the West Coast while serving as First Lady
To have a son win the Congressional Medal of Honor
White House Portrait: Daniel Huntington (currently in storage)

The More Colorful Facts

Astrological Sign: Virgo
Nicknames: Lemonade Lucy, Cousin Lute, Straight Laced Puritan, Mother Lucy
Childhood and Family Life: Lucy was the youngest of three children and the only daughter of Dr. James Webb and Maria Cook. Julia was named for her maternal grandmother; all four of her great-grandfathers fought in the Revolutionary War. After Webb's death, Julia and her family moved to Delaware, Ohio where her brothers were enrolled at Ohio Wesleyan. For six years, Lucy was the only female in its prep school. Two years later, she was graduated with high honors from Ohio Wesleyan Female College, the first First Lady to be graduated from college. She was a member of the debate team and elected to the Young Ladies' Lyceum. Her commencement essay was titled "The Influence of Christianity on National Prosperity."
Courtship and Marriage: Neighbors Maria Webb and Sophia Hayes decided that their two children, Lucy (age fourteen), and Rutherford (age twenty-three), would make a perfect match. They encouraged a friendship, but it wasn't until two years later that Lucy first appeared in Hayes's diary. Their courtship was one of poetry readings, picnics, and lively music. For her twentieth birthday, Hayes gave her five pieces of sheet music. Finally, the two young people became engaged, but waited 1½ years to marry while Hayes set up his law practice. The twenty-one-year old bride married the thirty-year-old groom in the front parlor of the Webb home at 141 Sixth Street in Cincinnati, Ohio. The Rev. Dr. Lorenzo Dow McCabe of Ohio Wesleyan officiated. The couple lived in Cincinnati, Washington, and at Spiegel Grove in Fremont, Ohio
Children: The Hayes had eight children, three of whom died in infancy. Birchard (1853–1926), Rutherford (1858–1927), and Scott (1871–1923) were all businessmen. Webb Cook (1856–1935) became the first presi-

dential son to win the Congressional Medal of Honor, for his heroics during the Spanish-American War, and established the Hayes Presidential Center in Fremont. Frances, known as Fanny (1867–1950), married and had one son.

Personal Notes: Lucy had a good sense of humor, a quick intellect, and was charming, gracious, and generous. She had a pleasant voice, loved to fish and ride horseback, and liked angel food cake and flowers, especially camellias. She loved animals of all kinds and called them her "Noah's collection." In 1877, she was presented with one of the first Siamese cats to be brought to the U.S. Lucy had Hayes build a pet cemetery at their Spiegel Grove home. She also collected autographs and had a six-volume collection of the works of famous poets, writers, and politicians. Her favorite books were the *Old Town Folks* series by Harriet Beecher Stowe. One of her good friends was the contemporary author, Ralph Waldo Emerson.

Soldier's Wife: During the Civil War, Lucy often visited her husband and his 23rd Ohio Volunteer troops. When she read in the paper that Hayes had been killed in the Battle of Cedar Creek, she spent a frantic two weeks searching for his body before finding him alive at a hospital in Maryland. She tended the wounded, mended their clothes, and wrote letters for them. An often-repeated story featured a green recruit, who was told by the other soldiers that the "lady in the white tent" had the job of sewing missing buttons on uniforms. But the joke was on them when the recruit came back, with his buttons intact, sewed on by the "general's wife." Lucy was honored many times by the men of the 23rd and was called "Mother Lucy."

Politician's Wife: After the war, Hayes became a congressman and later served two terms as governor of Ohio. Lucy was acknowledged as a talented hostess. She wore simple but tasteful dresses and her hair was parted in the middle. Instead of a hat, she preferred flowers in her hair. She was once introduced by President Ulysses S. Grant to Emperor Pedro III of Brazil as the "Queen of Ohio." As First Lady, she helped found a state home at Xenia for orphans of soldiers and sailors. The White House was also always open to veterans.

First Lady: Most of Lucy's activities as First Lady were overshadowed by the Hayes family belief in temperance. It has been said that she single-handedly made the Women's Christian Temperance Union respectable. Spirits were served only once in the Hayeses' entire four years at the White House. The occasion was a dinner in 1877 for Russian Grand Dukes Alexis and Constantin. When demands were placed on Hayes to serve liquor, he ordered oranges laced with San Croix rum flavoring placed in the punch. Four reasons have been given as to why they believed in temperance: (1) religious and moral convictions; (2)

desire to set a good example for their sons (and the country); (3) frugality on the part of Hayes (entertainment allowances had not been established yet by Congress); and (4) Hayes's desire to keep temperance in the Republican Party. Lucy renewed a past tradition of bringing Sunday worship to the White House. She lent her support to homes for the crippled, blind, mentally ill, and veterans. Lucy also started two traditions that continue today. The annual Easter Egg Roll on the White House lawn was begun when Congress complained the children were ruining the Capitol lawn. The other was an ornate scrapbook that described in detail all official functions, including menus and seating arrangements. This book is on display at the Hayes Presidential Center in Fremont, Ohio, and was most recently borrowed by the Reagan White House for duplication.

Post White House: In retirement, Lucy continued to support her special causes. She was a member of Lincoln Lodge No. 128, the Daughters of Rebekah. Her menagerie of animals included dog Gem, horse Dot, and goat Christopher Columbus. She was titular president of the Women's Home Missionary Society of the Methodist Episcopal Church. She was initiated as an honorary member of Kappa Kappa Gamma Sorority.

Death: Lucy died suddenly at age fifty-eight of a massive apoplectic stroke, suffered while watching a tennis match. It was probably caused by undiagnosed high blood pressure. The day of her funeral was one of total mourning in Fremont. She was buried in a gown of ivory cream in Oakwood Cemetery. Her favorite hymns, "My Jesus as Thou Wilt," "It is Well with My Soul," and "God Be With You 'till We Meet Again" were played. In 1915, the remains of Lucy and her husband were moved to Spiegel Grove.

Tribute: The Lucy Webb Hayes School of Nursing was founded at the American University, Washington, D.C. in 1891. It was dedicated as the Lucy Webb Hayes National Training School for Deaconesses & Missionaries.

LUCRETIA RUDOLPH GARFIELD

(1832–1918)

First Lady (1881)

The Straight Facts

Born: April 19, 1832
Birthplace: Garretsville, Ohio
Ancestry: English
Physical Characteristics: 5'3" tall, brown hair, brown eyes
Religion: Disciples of Christ
Husband: James Abram Garfield (1831–1881)
Date of Marriage: November 11, 1858
Place of Marriage: Hiram, Ohio
Children: Five sons, two daughters

Died: March 14, 1918
Place of Death: South Pasadena, California
Burial Place: Lakeview Cemetery, Cleveland, Ohio
White House Portrait: Mary Brenda Francklyn, White House Archives

The More Colorful Facts

Astrological Sign: Aries
Nickname: Crete
Childhood and Family Life: Lucretia was the daughter of Zebulon Rudolph, one of the founders of Hiram College, and Arabella Green Mason. Her childhood was spent near the family farm in Ohio. She was educated at Geauga Seminary and Western Reserve Eclectic Institute (later called Hiram College). At Hiram, she studied to be a teacher and revived the Ladies Literary Society.
Courtship and Marriage: She met James Garfield while both were students at Geauga Seminary. He would later be her Latin teacher at Hiram. Crete and Jim appeared together in a senior class production of *Mordecai and Haman,* as Queen Esther and King Ahasuerus. They dated others during their courtship and had a five-year understanding. He wrote letters to "Lucretia, My Sister" and she to "James, Very Kind Brother." They were finally married at the Rudolph home by Presbyterian minister Henry Hitchcock. The twenty-six-year-old bride wore a white dress with lace on the neck and short sleeves. The first years of their marriage were stormy as Garfield was not ready to settle down. They finally came to an understanding and developed a good relationship.
Children: They had seven children, two of whom died in infancy. Their sons became successful lawyers, politicians, and one was an architect.
Personal Notes: Lucretia was quiet, thoughtful, and loved to read the classics. She was also a good artist and loved to play bezique (a card game played with sixty-four cards that is similar to pinochle).
Soldier's/Politician's Wife: She assisted Garfield by doing research while he was studying law. She stayed at Lawnfield, their home at 8095 Mentor Avenue, Mentor, Ohio, while he fought in the Civil War as a general. When Garfield was elected to Congress, she and the children divided their time between Washington and Mentor. From 1861–1866, they lived together only twenty weeks. Lucretia was a private person who refused most social invitations. She also refused to pose for photographers, saying she was only Garfield's companion.
First Lady: As First Lady, Lucretia shunned most publicity. She did research at the Library of Congress before attempting to redecorate the White House. She never got the chance to finish the redecoration, how-

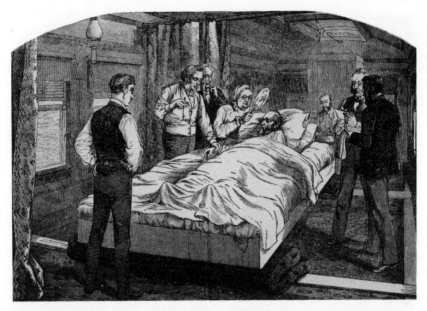

This engraving shows the dying Garfield, attended by his wife Lucretia.

ever. Less than three months after becoming First Lady, she was stricken with a 104° malarial fever and was sent with her three youngest children to Long Branch, New Jersey, to recuperate. While there, word came that Garfield had been shot. She rushed back to Garfield's side. She nursed him until he died eighty days later

Death: After Garfield's death, the family returned to Mentor and lived quietly. Lucretia was awarded a widow's pension of $5,000 a year and Garfield's one-year salary of $50,000. Her main project was to preserve Garfield's memory. She always referred to him as "The General" rather than "The President." All her correspondence was on black bordered stationery. She died at age eighty-six and is buried next to her husband in Lakeview Cemetery.

FRANCES FOLSOM CLEVELAND

(1864–1947)

First Lady (1886–1889; 1893–1897

The Straight Facts

Born: July 21, 1864
Birthplace: Buffalo, New York
Ancestry: English
Physical Characteristics: Chestnut hair, blue eyes
Religion: Presbyterian
Husbands: (1) (Stephen) Grover Cleveland (1837–1908)
          (2) Thomas Jex Preston, Jr. (1880–1955)

Date of Marriages: (1) June 2, 1886
(2) February 10, 1913
Place of Marriages: (1) Washington, D.C.
(2) Princeton, New Jersey
Children: (1) Two sons, three daughters
(2) None
Died: October 29, 1947
Place of Death: Baltimore, Maryland
Burial Place: Princeton Cemetery, Princeton, New Jersey
Firsts: To marry her husband in the White House
To serve two nonconsecutive terms as First Lady
To bear a child in the White House
To remarry after her husband's death
White House Portrait: Anders Zorn, East Wing Lobby

The More Colorful Facts

Astrological Sign: Cancer
Nicknames: Frank, Fairy Queen
Childhood and Family Life: Frances was the only child of attorney Oscar Folsom and Emma Cornelia Harmon. She attended Madame Brecker's Kindergarten, central school, and high school at Media, and went on to Wells College. Her father died when she was eleven and his law partner, Grover Cleveland, became her guardian. A bachelor, "Uncle Cleve" took care of "Frank" and her mother as if they were his own. It was rumored that Cleveland spent so much time with them was because he was taken with the charming widow.
Courtship and Marriage: After her graduation from Wells College in 1885, Frances and her mother went on a one-year grand tour of Europe. She and Cleveland had become secretly engaged prior to her trip and he felt it was important for her to learn about other cultures. Returning on the SS *Noordland,* they were met by Uncle Cleve, now president. Word of the engagement leaked out, and when Cleveland appeared on the docks, the band started to play "He's Going to Marry Yum Yum." Cleveland personally made the wedding arrangements and addressed invitations to the less than forty guests only four days before the ceremony. The wedding was originally to have taken place at the Buffalo home of Frances's grandfather, Col. John Folsom, but it was moved to the White House after Folsom died.

Together, the forty-nine-year-old groom and his twenty-one-year-old bride descended the stairs to the Blue Room for the ceremony. The bride wore a corded white satin gown, banded with orange blos-

President Grover Cleveland and Frances Folsom were married in a ceremony in The White House.

soms, a V-necked bodice, ¾-length sleeves, and a long sheer tulle veil. Her only jewelry was the sapphire-and-diamond engagement ring and the groom's wedding gift, a diamond necklace. The Marine Band, under the direction of John Philip Sousa, played "Desire," "I'm a Rose," and "Lohengrin." Under a horseshoe bower of flowers and bells, the Rev. Byron Sunderland of the First Presbyterian Church officiated, as the couple promised to love, honor, and keep (not obey). The groom's brother, the Rev. William Cleveland, pronounced the benediction. A nervous Cleveland forgot to kiss the bride after the ceremony. A private dinner was held, toasts were drunk (mineral water only for the bride), and the couple honeymooned in nearby Deer Park, Maryland.

Children: The Clevelands had five children. Oldest daughter Ruth (1891–1904), born between presidential terms, often played on the White House lawn. When too many people picked her up and passed her around, the nervous parents had the gates closed; critics then claimed she was deformed. A popular legend with no truth to it has the Baby Ruth candy bar named for her. Second daughter Esther (1893–1980) is the only presidential child to be born in the White House. Youngest daughter Marion (1895–) was born when the family was on vacation in

Buzzard's Bay, Massachusetts. They also had two sons, Richard (1897–1974), an attorney, and Francis (1903–).

Personal Notes: Frances played the piano and was an amateur photographer. She was fond of mockingbirds and canaries, which she kept as pets. She loved flowers, especially pansies and jonquils. When she was at Wells College, Cleveland often sent her flowers.

First Lady: Despite her youth, Frances easily stepped into the role of First Lady. Gracious and cordial, she held receptions three times a week. The most popular were the Saturday afternoon affairs for shopgirls. Often, after the affairs, her arms had to be massaged from shaking so many hands. She started a new fashion trend when she refused to wear a bustle. Cleveland purchased a home, nicknamed "Red Top" by the press, near Washington's Deer Park area, in the hope that they would get some privacy. The couple spent as much time there as at the White House. When Cleveland was defeated for reelection in 1888, Frances tearfully bid the staff goodbye and asked them to take care of everything as they would be back. Four years later they were back, the only presidential couple to serve two nonconsecutive terms. During the second term, Frances kept Cleveland's biggest secret, a cancer operation in which part of his jaw was removed.

Second Marriage: After leaving Washington for the second time, they moved to Princeton, New Jersey, where Cleveland became a professor. They raised their children in a home called Westland at 15 Hodge Street, near the campus. Frances was offered, but declined, the presidency of the National Society of the Daughters of the American Revolution because she did not want to subject herself to the political pressures the post entailed. Cleveland died in 1905 at age seventy-one. Eight years later, she married Princeton archeology professor Thomas Jex Preston, Jr. Then First Lady Helen Taft threw them a prewedding reception at the White House. Interestingly, after her second marriage, Frances signed documents and letters as "Frances F. Cleveland Preston." During the Depression, she led the Needlework Guild of America in a clothing drive for the poor.

Death: Frances died at age eighty-three in Baltimore and is buried in Princeton.

CAROLINE LAVINIA SCOTT HARRISON

(1832–1892)

First Lady (1889–1893)

The Straight Facts

Born: October 10, 1832
Birthplace: Oxford, Ohio
Ancestry: English
Physical Characteristics: Brown hair, brown eyes
Religion: Presbyterian
Husband: Benjamin Harrison (1833–1901)
Date of Marriage: October 20, 1853
Place of Marriage: New York, New York

Children: One son, one daughter
Died: October 25, 1889
Place of Death: Washington, D.C.
Burial Place: Crown Hill Cemetery, Indianapolis, Indiana
Firsts: To serve as president general of the National Society of the Daughters of the American Revolution
To erect the national Christmas tree
White House Portrait: Daniel Huntington, ground floor corridor

The More Colorful Facts

Astrological Sign: Libra
Nickname: Carrie
Childhood and Family Life: Caroline was the daughter of the Rev. Dr. John Witherspoon Scott and Mary Potts Neal. She attended Oxford Seminary, a female institute of higher learning of which her father was founder and president. Dr. Scott also taught at nearby Miami University.
Courtship and Marriage: She met Benjamin Harrison while he was a student at Miami University. Carrie helped her father at Oxford while Harrison completed his law studies during their engagement. The couple was married in the Scott family home by Caroline's father when both were twenty-one years of age. They lived in a boarding house in Oxford, then moved to Indianapolis where Harrison believed a lawyer could do better for his family.
Children: They had two children and, in 1861, a stillborn infant. Son Russell (1854–1936) served in the Spanish-American War and was a member of the Indiana House and Senate. Daughter Mary (1858–1930) had two children, one of whom, Benjamin Harrison McKee (or "Baby McKee" as he was dubbed by the press), was the nearly constant companion of his grandfather, the president.
Personal Notes: Caroline was an accomplished watercolor artist who painted china patterns. Always somewhere in her design was her trademark, a four-leaf clover. Carrie played the piano, sang, and did needlework. Active in the First Presbyterian Church, she taught Sunday school and played the organ. She also served as the president of the Indianapolis Women's Club. She is the only First lady to be born, marry, and die in the same month (October).
Politician's Wife: Outgoing Carrie was gay, stately, and poised. She was heavily engaged in charitable works in Indianapolis and Washington. She was supportive of his career but against her husband, the senator,

running for president. She was afraid he would die in office like his grandfather, ninth president William Henry Harrison.

First Lady: As First Lady, Caroline renovated the White House family quarters. In addition to her children and their families, Carrie's father and widowed niece Mary Scott Dimmick lived with them. She submitted designs to Congress to expand the executive mansion which housed numerous agencies and commissions, but it wasn't until sixty years later that new rooms were added. She established order in the kitchens, eliminated waste, and had a conservatory built so that plants from the White House could be used for receptions. Caroline was fond of hothouse flowers and it is reported that at one reception, over 5,000 plants were used. Orchids were her favorite flower. She also broke tradition by carrying flowers in receiving lines, thereby saving her fingers from thousands of squeezes and handshakes. She became the first president general of the Daughters of the American Revolution when the Sons of the American Revolution would not let women join. When Johns Hopkins Medical School was started, she agreed to lend support only if women were given equal admittance. With the assistance of her niece, she placed china arrangements from past administrations on display. Caroline also wanted to make corn the national vegetable.

Death: In the midst of the 1892 summer campaign Carrie was taken ill. Doctors diagnosed cancer and recommended a trip to the Adirondacks in the hopes that the higher elevation would help her breathing. She died in the White House at age sixty, less than four months after becoming ill. Her wake was held in the East Room and burial was in Indianapolis at the Crown Hill Cemetery.

IDA SAXTON MCKINLEY

(1847–1907)

First Lady (1897–1901)

The Straight Facts

Born: June 8, 1847
Birthplace: Canton, Ohio
Ancestry: English
Physical Characteristics: Auburn hair, blue eyes
Religion: Methodist-Episcopalian
Husband: William McKinley (1843–1901)
Date of Marriage: January 25, 1871
Place of Marriage: Canton, Ohio
Children: Two daughters
Died: May 26, 1907
Place of Death: Canton, Ohio
Burial Place: Westlawn Cemetery, Canton, Ohio
White House Portrait: Emily Drayton Taylor, Treaty Room

The More Colorful Facts

Astrological Sign: Gemini

Childhood and Family Life: Ida was the spoiled, intelligent oldest daughter
of banker James Asbury Saxton and Katherine DeWalt. She attended
school at Miss Sandford's in Cleveland, Ohio, and Miss Eastman's
Brooke Hall Seminary in Media, Pennsylvania. Raised in the Presbyterian Church, she was a Sunday School teacher and supporter of missionaries in India and the Philippines. She and sister Mary "Pina"
(pronounced Piney) took an eight-month grand tour of Europe in 1869,
accompanied by Miss Jeannete Alexander. Upon their return, Ida went
to work at her father's bank as a cashier.

Courtship and Marriage: She met Major William McKinley during a picnic
at Meyer's Lake, introduced by his schoolteacher sister, Anna. The
dashing war hero won the hand of the twenty-four-year-old beauty over
other eligible suitors. They were the first couple married in the new
First Presbyterian Church that her father and grandfather helped
build. The ceremony was performed by her pastor, Rev. Edward Buck-
ingham and McKinley's Methodist minister, the Rev. Dr. John Endsley. Brother Abner McKinley served as best man and Pina was maid of
honor. In a twist of fate, Abner would later marry Endsley's daughter
Anna and Pina would marry one of the ushers, Marshall Barbour. The
McKinleys honeymooned in New York and the bride's father gave
them a home as a wedding present. They were most devoted to each
other and she called him "My Precious."

Children: Two daughters, Katherine and Ida, died in infancy. Ida would not
permit their clothes or toys to be thrown away and kept them with her.
She became attached to the children of others and became lovingly
known as "Aunt McKinley."

Personal Notes: The deaths of the children and her mother within a three-
year period broke Ida's spirit. She suffered from nervous disorders
which developed into epilepsy. She also contracted phlebitis (inflama-
tion of the veins) in her legs. A compulsive needleworker, it is said that
she made thousands of pairs of slippers for relatives and various hospitals. She was fond of euchre, cribbage, the poems of Tennyson, and she
collected fine laces.

Politician's Wife: Frail health and the need to walk with the aid of a cane did
not stop Ida from accompanying McKinley on most of his travels. In
Washington, they lived at the Old Ebbitt House. Her gentle demeanor
made her a favorite in political circles and the couple were frequent
guests at the Hayes White House. McKinley had served in Hayes's
Civil War regiment; Ida even substituted for Lucy while the latter was

Ida McKinley (in white) with President McKinley (second from right) at the Pan-American Exposition in Buffalo, New York, on September 5, 1901, the day before he was shot.

on a two-week vacation. When McKinley was governor of Ohio, they lived at the Neil House Hotel, directly across from the state Capitol. Every morning before entering the building, he would stop, turn, and tip his hat to her; every afternoon at precisely 3 P.M., he would go to the window and wave his handkerchief at her and she would be in the front hotel window waving back.

First Lady: McKinley broke precedent by seating Ida at his right at dinner so he could care for her if she had an epileptic seizure. If stricken, he would gently place a large handkerchief over her face, wait for the seizure to cease, remove the cloth, and then proceed as if nothing happened. Entertaining was limited to small dinners, afternoon teas, and a few official receptions. The practice of ranking cabinet members over diplomats at receptions began. Ida would receive guests seated on a thronelike chair, flanked by cabinet wives or relatives who would shake hands with visitors. Her poor constitution rarely allowed her to eat the lavish foods prepared for these dinners, so she generally ate off a plate of crackers. She accompanied McKinley to Buffalo for the ill-fated Pan Am Exposition in 1901 and was constantly at his side during the eight days of his confinement after being shot. Many were surprised she held up so well and she made nearly all the burial decisions herself.

Death: Ida lived quietly for six more years, attended by maid Clara Thurin, and was in constant ill health. She visited McKinley's grave nearly every day. She died at age sixty in Canton and is buried next to her husband and their daughters in Westlawn Cemetery.

EDITH KERMIT CAROW ROOSEVELT

(1861–1948)

First Lady (1901–1909)

The Straight Facts

Born: August 6, 1861
Birthplace: Norwich, Connecticut
Ancestry: English
Physical Characteristics: 5'7" tall, 125 lbs., brown hair, blue eyes
Religion: Episcopalian
Husband: Theodore Roosevelt (1858–1919)
Date of Marriage: December 2, 1886

Place of Marriage: London, England
Children: Four sons, one daughter
Died: September 30, 1948
Place of Death: Oyster Bay, New York
Burial Place: Young's Cemetery, Oyster Bay, New York
Firsts: To be born in Connecticutt
　　　　To travel outside the U.S. while First Lady
White House Portrait: Theobald Chartran, Family Dining Room

The More Colorful Facts

Astrological Sign: Leo
Nicknames: Edie, Spotless Edie, Mother of the Regiment
Childhood and Family Life: Edith was the eldest daughter of Charles Carow and Gertrude Elizabeth Tyler. She had one sister, Emily. She was born in the Carow ancestral home in Connecticut. Her family ancestry can be traced back to the 1600s and among relatives were Puritan Jonathan Edwards and author Edith Wharton. The Carow family was well-to-do and they traveled in the same social circles as that of her future husband. She attended Miss Comstock's Academy and took dancing lessons at Mr. Dodsworth's School for Dancing and Deportment. She gained an appreciation of the Bible from her Grandfather Tyler, who offered gifts to any child who could recite the book of Proverbs.
Courtship and Marriage: She grew up near the family of Theodore Roosevelt. She was a constant companion of the Roosevelt children and even attended kindergarten at their home. In a photograph of the 1865 funeral procession for Abraham Lincoln through New York City can be , seen young Theodore Roosevelt, who was seven years old. Had the picture been taken a few minutes earlier, it would also have shown four-year-old Edith. He had locked her in a closet because she distracted him from watching the parade.

　　Throughout their childhood, Edith and Roosevelt often went hiking, swimming, and rowing together. At age seventeen, he painted her name on a rowboat. Before Roosevelt entered his second year of college, they quarreled. Shortly thereafter he met Alice Lee, and it was a heartbroken Edith who attended their wedding. After Alice died in 1884, Roosevelt left his infant daughter with his sister, Anna, known as Bamie, and went into seclusion at Elkhorn Ranch in the Dakota Territory. When Roosevelt returned in 1885, he and Edith tried to avoid one another but it was inevitable that they would run into each other. A chance meeting at Bamie's rekindled their friendship, and love developed.

When Edith went to live with her mother and sister in England, Roosevelt proposed and sent engagement gifts of a ring, watch, and pearl necklace. They married in London at St. George's Church. Emily Carow and Sir Cecil Spring-Rice were the attendants. The twenty-five-year-old bride wore a Valenciennes lace gown with an orange-blossom veil; the groom completed his outfit with bright orange gloves. The Rev. Dr. Charles Cambidge, Canon of York, officiated and the couple honeymooned in Europe.

Children: It was Edith who insisted that Roosevelt's daughter Alice live with them. Together, Edith and Roosevelt had five children. Theodore, Jr. (1887–1944), Kermit (1889–1943), and Quentin (1897–1918) all died while in the service of their country. Theodore, Jr. won the Congressional Medal of Honor. Archie (1894–1979) served in both world wars. Ethel (1891–1977) married Dr. Richard Derby. The antics of the Roosevelt children, their father, and their pets are well known. Never before (or since) has the White House seen an alligator in the bathtub, ponies in the elevators, or snakes in the reception room. Edith called Roosevelt her sixth child because he was just as playful as the children. When the children asked their mother how she knew so much, she told them it came from a military gentleman—"General Information."

Personal Notes: Edith was an athletic woman who enjoyed most outdoor exercises including hiking, rowing, climbing, swimming, and riding. Among her favorite mounts were Yagenka and Nicollette. Like most Carows, she was an avid reader; her father was once a shareholder in the New York Library Society. Her favorite author was Shakespeare, especially the plays *As You Like It, Macbeth,* and *Romeo and Juliet.* She also enjoyed sewing, needlework, and was partial to animals.

Politician's Wife: Edith preferred staying at home, raising the children, and handling the family finances while Roosevelt climbed the political ladder. When she was called on to entertain, she did so graciously, with gentleness and warmth. Political issues were not to be discussed at the dinner table. They made one visit to Elkhorn Ranch but stayed mostly in New York City and Oyster Bay. In February 1894, they were invited to dinner at the White House as the guests of President and Mrs. Cleveland. Roosevelt escorted Mrs. Cleveland into dinner and Edith was escorted by Richard W. Gildy, editor of *Century* Magazine. She wrote in her diary that it would probably be her only trip to the White House.

When Roosevelt ran for vice president, Edith appeared infrequently with him on the campaign trail. Only after the election would she allow her picture to appear in the newspaper. In the seven months Roosevelt served as vice president, Edith rarely went to Washington and met Mrs. McKinley only a few times.

First Lady: As First Lady, she put her skills of making order out of chaos to good use. It was a somber new First Lady who entered the White House after the death of William McKinley, but a noisy, boisterous group of children. The latter arrived with trunks, toys, and any pets that fit into cages or pockets; the rest would be shipped later.

Edith preferred overseeing the housekeeping of the White House herself and hired caterers for state dinners. The Roosevelts entertained often but not lavishly. Lady diners always found a fresh flower at their place settings. Musicales were held every Friday during the season. In their first full year, they held 180 events in six months.

To keep up with the constant round of events, she hired the first social secretary to serve a First Lady, Belle Hagner. Miss Hagner was also responsible for keeping detailed records of menus, setting arrangements, and protocol in the hope that they would be beneficial to future First Ladies. Together, Edith and Belle took inventory of various china patterns used by past administrations.

Edith's china service was 120 place settings of English Wedgewood that was creamy white with a two-inch-wide colonial motif border incorporating the Great Seal of the United States enameled in red, brown, and yellow. After Quentin rode his wagon through the portrait of former First Lady Lucy Hayes, Edith had all the portraits of former presidents and their First Ladies inventoried and put on display. The three social highlights of her tenure were the debuts of daughters Alice and Ethel and the wedding of Alice to Congressman Nicholas Longworth of Ohio.

Edith was also a help to Roosevelt during his presidency. She helped open mail, answered letters, and clipped newspaper articles for him to read. She also watched his health, supervised his meals, and reminded him that bedtime was 10:30 P.M. Edith was consulted when two wings were added to the White House. The State Dining Room, which previously held only one hundred people, was also expanded.

Post White House: Roosevelt vowed not to run for reelection in 1908. Shortly after leaving the White House, the Roosevelts sailed to Europe on the SS *Crete* and returned the next year on the SS *Kaiserin Auguste Victoria*. Edith busied herself with the Christ Church Needlework Guild and Episcopal church affairs. In 1911, she was thrown from a horse and was in a coma for nine days. As a result, she lost her sense of taste and smell.

Following Roosevelt's death, Edith traveled extensively and called her travels the Odyssey of a Grandmother. In the first eight years of widowhood, she went to London, Paris (to see Quentin's grave), Spain, Italy, Grenada, Africa, and South and Central America. During Prohibition, she continued to serve liquor at her dinners because she did not believe Congress had the right to dictate personal habits. In 1924, she wrote a study of her family called *American Backlogs.* In 1927, she and Kermit co-authored *Cleared for Strange Ports,* a travelbook. She was active in the Republican party and the Edith Carow Roosevelt Republican Club was named for her. In 1932, she actively campaigned for Herbert Hoover.

Death: In her later years, Edith was plagued by ill health. She broke a hip at age seventy-four. She died at age eighty-seven of arteriosclerosis (hardening of the arterial walls). She survived her husband by twenty-seven years and outlived three of her sons. She chose the music to be played at her funeral—Beethoven's Ninth Symphony ("Ode to Joy"), "The Son of God," and "Love Divine." She is buried next to her husband in Young's Cemetery in Oyster Bay. Surviving son Archie wrote her epitapth "Everything she did was for the happiness of others."

HELEN HERRON TAFT

(1861–1943)

First Lady 1909–1913

The Straight Facts

Born: September 2, 1861
Birthplace: Cincinnati, Ohio
Ancestry: English
Physical Characteristics: 5'7" tall, brown hair, gray-blue eyes
Religion: Episcopalian
Husband: William Howard Taft (1857–1930)
Date of Marriage: June 19, 1886
Place of Marriage: Cincinnati, Ohio
Children: Two sons, one daughter
Died: May 22, 1943

Place of Death: Washington, D.C.
Burial Place: Arlington National Cemetery, Arlington, Virginia
Firsts: To ride with her husband in the inaugural parade
    To introduce twin beds to the White House
    To publish memoirs
    To be buried in Arlington National Cemetery
White House Portrait: Bror Kronstrand, Grand Staircase

The More Colorful Facts

Astrological Sign: Virgo
Nickname: Nellie
Childhood and Family Life: Helen was one of eleven children of John Williamson Herron and Harriet Collins. Her father attended Miami University with twenty-third president Benjamin Harrison and was a law partner of nineteenth president Rutherford B. Hayes. The Herron family were often guests at the Hayes White House and named a daughter after Lucy Hayes. After one visit, seventeen-year-old Helen, who had vowed never to marry and planned on joining a convent, decided to marry a man who would be president.She graduated from Miss Nourse's School (nicknamed the Nursery) and attended the University of Cincinnati.
Courtship and Marriage: Schoolteacher Helen met attorney William Howard Taft at a sledding party on Mt. Auburn near Cincinnati. She was eighteen years old. For the next six years they went on picnics, acted in plays together, and attended dances. They became serious after Helen, worried that she was too frivolous, organized a "salon" for intellectual and economic topics and Taft attended almost every session. His proposal of marriage was rejected twice. After making him wait for over one month, Nellie accepted his May 1, 1885 proposal. During their one-year engagement, Taft showered her with many gifts including a set of dumbbells which he said would would help her rheumatism. The twenty-five-year-old bride married her 250-pound, twenty-nine-year-old groom in the parlor of her parents' home. She carried a bouquet of sweet peas and lillies of the valley. The Rev. D.N.A. Hoge of Zanesville, Ohio, officiated, just as he had done for her parents. The newlyweds took a one-hundred-day honeymoon to New York and Europe. They sailed on the SS *City of Chester* and visited Great Britain, Scotland, France, and Holland. They returned on the SS *City of Chicago,* which collided with a fishing smack in the fog. There were no injuries but much of Helen's Delft china was broken in the collision.

Children: The Tafts had three children. Robert Alphonso (1889–1953) was a leading statesman and was called "Mr. Republican." Helen Taft Manning (1891–1987) helped her mother in the White House and served as president of Bryn Mawr College. Charles Phelps (1897–1983) was a mayor of Cincinnati.

Personal Notes: Helen loved to dance, played the piano, and loved music of all kinds including the classics, opera, band music, and theatre songs. She was fluent in French and more than passable in Spanish. She took art classes, enjoyed card games, and was known to join Taft in a game of poker and a glass of beer. Her favorite flowers were Killarney roses, orchids, and daisies.

Politician's Wife: In the first thirteen years of marrige, the Tafts lived in Cincinnati, Washington, and Cincinnati again as Taft assumed various judicial posts. During this time, both became active in civic affairs. Nellie was a cofounder of the Cincinnati Symphony Orchestra Association. In 1899, Taft was appointed governor general of the Philippines. The entire family sailed April 17, 1900 on the USS *Hancock* for a four-year stay. The energetic and quick-witted Helen soon picked up the customs of Philippine protocol and became a valuable assistant to Taft. Tactful and diplomatic, with charming ways, she was able to make the Filipinos understand that they were there to help them. Garden parties given at the Malacanan Palace by the Tafts were well attended and very successful. She traveled with Taft to Rome when the sale of the Philippines was negotiated and had a private audience with the Pope. Helen also visited Panama with Taft during the construction of the Panama Canal and went to Cuba following the Spanish-American War.

First Lady: Helen wanted Taft to become president; he wanted to be chief justice of the Supreme Court. In 1908, Theodore Roosevelt handpicked Taft to be his successor, and four months later, Helen's dream was realized. The entire Taft and Herron families attended the swearing-in ceremonies. Twelve-year-old Charlie Taft brought along a copy of *Treasure Island* to read because he thought the ceremony would be boring. Following the ceremony, Helen broke precedent by riding in a limousine with her husband in the inaugural parade. She then went about setting up the White House in her own analytical and orderly manner. Liveried footmen served meals. Mrs. Elizabeth Jaffray was hired as housekeeper. Helen also hired financier J. P. Morgan's Swedish cook. Family cow Pauline Wayne grazed on the White House lawn. The family quarters were redecorated to resemble the Malacanan Palace. She used fresh flowers, ferns, and palms from the White House conservatory for centerpieces and ornaments.

Two months into her tenure, Helen suffered a stroke while on her way to Mt. Vernon on the SS *Sylph*. It affected the left side of her face and her speech; Taft painstakingly taught her how to talk again. During her year-long confinement, daughter Helen assisted with the few social functions held. She served as guest hostess for a dinner honoring Prince and Princess Fushimi of Japan. However, Helen hosted her daughter's debut at an afternoon tea for over 1,200 guests. The Tafts inaugurated the custom of mingling with guests after dinner, and the guests were free to leave when they wished. Previous presidential couples left right after dinner. The Tafts celebrated their twenty-fifth wedding anniversary in 1911 in a very ornate ceremony. Ever the romantic, Helen hosted a private dinner for former First Lady Frances Cleveland and her fiancé, Thomas J. Preston, in 1913.

Helen is best known for two feats as First lady. She was the first to attend cabinet meetings. She claimed she did not go to set policy, but because the obese Taft suffered from narcolepsy (brief attacks of deep sleep) and she wanted to keep him awake. Helen is also responsible for the planting of 3,500 Yoshino (single white flower) cherry trees around the Tidal Basin in Washington. The trees were a gift from the mayor of Tokyo, Yukio Ozaki, and his wife. The design for the Basin park was copied from Manila's Luneta, an oval drive with bandstands on either side. The Marine Band played at the first concert with President and Mrs. Taft in attendance.

Justice's Wife: After leaving the White House in 1909, the Tafts moved to New Haven, Connecticut, where Taft became a professor of law at Yale University. In 1921, President Warren G. Harding appointed Taft to his dream post, the chief justice of the Supreme Court. He served for nine years and they lived at 5 DuPont Circle. In retirement, Helen played golf, joined a book club, and attended plays. She also penned her memoirs, *Recollections of Full Years.*

Death: Helen lived thirteen years after her husband and died at age eighty-two in her DuPont Circle home. She is buried next to her husband in Arlington National Cemetery, the only First Lady to rest there.

ELLEN LOUISE AXSON WILSON

(1860–1914)

First Lady 1913–1914

The Straight Facts

Born: May 15, 1860
Birthplace: Savannah, Georgia
Ancestry: English
Physical Characteristics: 5'6" tall, brown hair, brown eyes
Religion: Presbyterian
Husband: (Thomas) Woodrow Wilson (1856–1924)
Date of Marriage: June 24, 1886
Place of Marriage: Savannah, Georgia

Children: Three daughters
Died: August 6, 1914
Place of Death: Washington, D.C.
Burial Place: Myrtle Hill Cemetery, Rome, Georgia
Firsts: To be born in Georgia
　　　To have a cause while First Lady
Official Portrait: Unknown artist, Carnegie Library, Rome, Georgia

The More Colorful Facts

Astrological Sign: Taurus
Nicknames: Miss Ellie Lou, Eileen
Childhood and Family Life: Ellen was the daughter of the Rev. Samuel E. Axson and Margaret Hoyt. Her father was a third-generation minister and she was brought up in a very religious atmosphere. She attended local schools, including the Female Seminary in Rome, Georgia. She spent 1883 studying painting at the Art Students League in New York City.
Courtship and Marriage: As a child, she met "Tommy" Woodrow Wilson who was a cousin of her friend, Jessie. They were reintroduced when Wilson, now a graduate of Princeton University, again came to visit. After only eleven meetings, he proposed. The marriage was postponed while Wilson completed his doctorate and Ellen finished her art studies. Almost daily during the engagement, they exchanged long love letters, a practice they continued when separated during married life. They were married at the home of her paternal grandfather in Savannah. Wilson's father, the Rev. Joseph R. Wilson, and her grandfather, the Rev. Isaac Axson, officiated. The groom was twenty-nine, the bride twenty-five, and they honeymooned in North Carolina at the Waynesville Resort.
Children: The Wilsons had three daughters. Margaret (1886–1944) was a singer who entertained troops in World War I. She never married and died in India where she had gone to seek inner peace. Jessie (1887–1933) married lawyer Francis B. Sayre in the White House in 1913. Their son would became rector of the Washington National Cathedral. Youngest daughter Eleanor (1889–1967) married widower William Gibbs McAdoo, who was her father's secretary of treasury in 1914. All three girls loved to join tours of the White House and to make snide remarks about "the ugly Wilson girls," much to the dismay of unsuspecting tourists. They would laugh with glee when the crowds finally discovered who they were.
Personal Notes: Ellen has been described as talented, energetic, and bright. She was a good household manager who grew vegetables, designed and

sewed her own clothes, and helped her husband and their girls with their studies. Fluent in German, she taught the language to Wilson and helped translate articles for him. Ellen also proofread all his books, articles, and speeches.

Politician's Wife: It was Ellen who first urged her scholarly college president husband to enter politics. She became active in Democratic affairs, entertained party leaders, cultivated campaign workers, and rehearsed speeches with him. He frequently discussed issues with her before introducing them publicly.

First Lady: Ellen stood on a chair to watch her husband's swearing-in ceremony since no provisions were made as to where she should stand. Her short tenure as First Lady was marked by gay parties, the White House weddings of two daughters, and concern for others. A charming hostess, she gave twice-a-week receptions, preferring informal garden parties to lavish receptions. A longtime volunteer for those less fortunate, she was a member of the Board of Associated Charities and worked hard to improved housing for the impoverished in the nation's capital.

Death: In 1914, Ellen suffered a bad fall. Three months later, it was discovered that she had Bright's disease (a kidney disease). Congress rushed through passage of her pet project, the "Alley Bill" or "Mrs. Wilson's Bill," which provided decent housing in the slums. She died in the White House at age fifty-four, only six months after becoming ill. She was buried in her hometown of Rome, Georgia.

EDITH BOLLING GALT WILSON

(1872–1961)
First Lady (1915–1921)

The Straight Facts

Born: October 15, 1872
Birthplace: Wytheville, Virginia
Ancestry: English, American Indian
Physical Characteristics: 5'9"tall, brown hair, gray eyes
Religion: Episcopalian
Husbands: (1) Norman Galt (?-1908)
(2) Woodrow Wilson (1856–1924)
Date of Marriages: (1) April 30, 1896?
(2) December 18, 1915
Place of Marriages: (1) Wytheville, Virginia
(2) Washington, D.C.
Children: None

Died: December 28, 1961
Place of Death: Washington, D.C.
Burial Place: Washington National Cathedral, Washington, D.C.
Firsts: To travel overseas as First Lady
To purchase American-made china for the White House
To die on her husband's birthday
White House Portrait: Adolph Muller-Ury, East Wing Reception Room

The More Colorful Facts

Astrological Sign: Libra
Nicknames: Madame President, Gray Spider, The First Lady of the World
Childhood and Family Life: Edith was the seventh of eleven children of Circuit Court judge William Holcombe Bolling and Sallie White. Her grandmother seven times removed was the Indian princess, Pocahontas. The family were members of the Virginia aristocracy who had lost their fortune during the Civil War. Because money was scarce, the children were educated at home. A grandmother taught her to read, write, and speak French. Finances improved and she was able to attend one year at Martha Washington College in nearby Abingdon, and one year at the Powell School in Richmond.
First Husband: On a visit to her sister, Mrs. Alexander Galt, she met the younger brother-in-law. Norman Galt was several years Edith's senior and thoroughly captivated by her. After a four-year courtship, they were married. She was twenty-four when they moved to Washington after the honeymoon. He worked at the family jewelry store, and they bought a home at 1308 12th Street NW. Galt soon became owner of the store and, when he died, Edith inherited the business. She ran it for two years before selling it to employees. She invested the proceeds, traveled abroad, and took in Alice Gertrude (Altrude) Gordon, the orphaned daughter of a friend. She was also the first woman in Washington to own an electric car.
Courtship and Marriage: A frequent visitor to the Galt home was Admiral Cary Grayson, the White House physician who hoped to marry Altrude. He introduced Edith to President Woodrow Wilson's cousin, Helen Woodrow Bones, who had come to live in the White House after the death of the First Lady. Soon Edith and Helen were great friends. They took walks together, played golf, and rode around town in the electric car. In March 1915, Helen invited Edith to tea at the White House. Edith only accepted after Helen promised the president would not be there. Windswept and with muddy shoes, Edith literally walked out of the elevator and into the president, who had returned early from playing golf.

Wilson joined them for tea and was immediately captivated by the smiling widow. That evening, he sent her flowers and the courtship began. They took walks, rode, played golf, and cruised on the presidential yacht. He had a private telephone line installed between the White House and her 12th Street home. Within two months he proposed. Edith resisted, claiming it was too soon after his first wife's death. She finally agreed in October and the marriage was set for December. Their first public appearance together was at a World Series baseball game between the Boston Red Sox and the Philadelphia Athletics. They exchanged daily letters; he called her "Little Girl" and she wrote to "My Dearest One."

A small wedding was planned with only family invited. Edith asked an Episcopal bishop to perform the ceremony and informed him it was to be small and no guests outside family were to be invited. Shortly before the ceremony, the bishop wrote that his wife would be attending also. Edith told him no outsiders and that his services would no longer be needed. Two days later, the Rev. Dr. Herbert S. Smith, pastor of Edith's St. Mary's Episcopal Church, and the Rev. Dr. James H. Taylor, pastor of Wilson's Central Presbyterian Church, officiated at the wedding. The forty-three-year-old bride was given away by her mother. She wore a plain black velvet gown with orchids at the waist and carried a sprig of lilies of the valley. Her large black velvet hat was covered with exotic flowers. The ring was made of pure gold, donated by the people of California.

The couple honeymooned in Hot Springs, Virginia. After their first night together, the president sang "Oh, You Beautiful Doll" to her in their private railroad car. Wilson's three daughters approved of the marriage; they knew how lonely he had been after their mother's death.

Children: During her first marriage, Edith had several miscarriages; the last was so severe she could not have children.

Personal Notes: Edith played the piano, could sing, and had a photographic memory. She was a good golfer and regularly beat the president. Always game for a new adventure, she learned to ride a bicycle in the basement of the White House. Her favorite colors were violet and turquoise. Her favorite meal was Lobster Newburgh.

First Lady: The Wilsons entered the White House in 1916. Without ever having attended a White House dinner, Edith gave a reception for 3,000 guests. When taking up residence, the only furniture brought from her 12th Street home were her piano, sewing machine, and rolltop desk. Aides (and Edith) were afraid Wilson would lose his bid for re-election because of his marrying so soon after the death of his first wife. It was close, but he was awarded a second term.

Edith became Wilson's closest confidant and he regularly discussed issues with her. Edith entertained in a limited fashion, preferring smaller dinners to large, lavish receptions. She employed Edith Benham Helm as her social secretary. She purchased a 700-piece set of American Lenox china featuring the presidential seal motif with a gold rim. America's entry into World War I also limited opportunities to entertain. During the war, she closed the White House to all but official guests, sewed clothes for the soldiers on her old sewing machine, volunteered for the Red Cross, and permitted sheep to graze on the White House lawn. The wool was then sold to support the war effort. Like other American families, the Wilsons participated in wheatless, meatless, gasless, and heatless days. The Navy Department asked her to rename eighty-nine German ships that had become spoils of war. Edith found it a difficult task and often used Indian names.

After the war, Edith went with Wilson to Paris for the signing of the peace treaty. She witnessed the signing, refused to curtsy to Queen Mary, and gloried in the warm reception given to Wilson. In the U.S., sentiment did not run in favor of Wilson's Fourteen Points, the cornerstone of the League of Nations. Among the leaders opposed to the idea was Henry Cabot Lodge of Massachusetts. Wilson decided to take the issue to the people and set out on an exhausting whistlestop tour. Upon his return, he fell ill.

Stewardship: On October 2, 1919, Wilson suffered a paralytic stroke. Dr. Grayson called in experts who agreed the situation was very serious but not fatal. The notion that the president resign was quickly discarded. Neurologist Dr. Francis Dercum advised complete bed rest with no disturbances. According to Edith's biography, *My Memoirs,* published in 1939, she was told "Have everything come to you, weigh the importance of each, consult with department heads, and free him from worry." She did exactly that.

For six weeks, no one knew the condition of the president. After a while, his private secretary was allowed to visit once a day. No public official, including the vice-president, was allowed in the room. Edith read dispatches, referred matters to cabinet officers, took Wilson's dictation, and protected him from the stress of political problems. She claimed to have made no decisions regarding public policy. But she admitted that Wilson never read, never saw, never listened to, or never signed anything she didn't approve of first. Finally, a "smelling committee," lead by Senator Albert Fall, was allowed to see Wilson. They had been sent to "smell out" the situation and disclose the president's condition to Congress. Fall told Wilson that he had been praying for him; Wilson asked "which way."

Wilson made a slow, painful recovery and only walked again with the aid of two canes. The press called it a "Petticoat Government" or "Mrs. Wilson's Regency." But those who have done extensive research on the subject conclude that she literally followed the doctor's orders in order to aid her husband's recovery, and no more. She did, and he lived five more years.

Edith Wilson, in 1955, together with Bess Truman and Eleanor Roosevelt.

Post White House: When they left the White House, the Wilsons moved to 2340 S Street NW. Following the Scottish tradition, Wilson presented Edith with the keys and a piece of sod. Wilson was a semi-invalid, and to make him feel comfortable, Edith had a replica of his Lincoln bed made for their new home. When Wilson died in 1924, Edith told his old political enemy, Senator Henry Cabot Lodge, that he would be persona non grata at the funeral.

The next thirty-seven years were spent preserving and promoting Wilson's memory. Edith served as a director of the Woodrow Wilson Foundation, helped dedicate the Woodrow Wilson National Shrine, and participated in the 1956 Woodrow Wilson Centennial Celebration. She had all of his letters copyrighted and personally answered all letters, no matter how small or trivial.

Edith traveled extensively, and when in Europe, always attended League of Nations meetings. She was an avid reader, loved bridge, and played golf. Hard of hearing, she was forced to wear a hearing aid. One of her last public appearances was at the inauguration of John F. Kennedy. One of eight First Ladies present, she wore a purple suit and carried a flask of bourbon to help ward off the cold.

Death: She died at age eighty-nine in her home, which was donated to the National Historic Trust in her will. She is buried in the Washington National Cathedral, one crypt below her husband.

FLORENCE MABEL KLING DE WOLFE HARDING

(1860–1924)

First Lady (1921–1923)

The Straight Facts

Born: August 15, 1860
Birthplace: Marion, Ohio
Ancestry: English, German
Physical Characteristics: 5'5" tall, brown hair, blue eyes
Religion: Baptist
Husbands: (1) Henry A. (Pete) De Wolfe (1858–1894)
(2) Warren Gamaliel Harding (1865–1923)

Date of Marriages: (1) March 1880; divorced in 1886
(2) July 8, 1891
Place of Marriages: (1) Marion, Ohio
(2) Marion, Ohio
Children: (1) One son
(2) None
Died: November 21, 1924
Place of Death: Marion, Ohio
Burial Place: Harding Memorial, Marion, Ohio
Firsts: To serve as First Lady in her sixties
Divorcé to serve as First Lady
To vote for her husband for President
White House Portrait: Philip de Laszlo, Queen's Bedroom

The More Colorful Facts

Astrological Sign: Leo
Nicknames: Flossie, the Duchess
Childhood and Family Life: Florence was the youngest of three and the only daughter of banker Amos Kling and Louisa Bouton. Displeased at having a daughter, Kling raised her as he did his boys. A strict disciplinarian, Kling locked the doors to the house at 11 P.M. and Florence often spent the night at the home of a girlfriend. Because she was a natural musician, he allowed her to attend the Cincinnati Conservatory of Music.
First Husband: She eloped with next-door neighbor Pete De Wolfe in 1880. He was an alcoholic who could not keep a job and his father was constantly bailing him out of trouble. The couple separated in 1884 and the divorce became final two years later. Pete died of "laryngitis" caused by alcohol in 1893, broke and disowned by his family. Amos Kling never accepted the marriage, and when it collapsed, he would only help his daughter and her child if Florence consented to move in with him and retake her maiden name. She refused and made a living by giving piano lessons. Her mother (behind Amos' back) and her DeWolfe in-laws helped her with expenses. Among her students was Charity (Chat) Harding, the sister of newsman Warren G. Harding.
Courtship and Marriage: It is probable that Florence and "Wurr'n" met prior to Chat's lessons. She was the aggressor in the relationship and chased Harding for two years. They were married in the front parlor of the home they designed together at 380 Mt. Vernon Avenue, Marion. The house was built by Captain Jacob Apt. Amos Kling again dis-

owned his daughter, believing the Hardings below them socially and resurrecting an old rumor that there was Negro blood in the family. He refused to attend the ceremony; her mother slipped in before the ceremony started and left just as quickly when it was over, before her daughter saw her. It would be seven years before Amos would talk to Florence again and fifteen years before he stepped foot in her home.

Children: Eugene Marshall De Wolfe (1880–1914) was born six months after his parents' hasty wedding. From age four, he lived with his maternal grandparents as Marshall Kling, attending Marion High School for four years but not graduating. He married and tried the newspaper trade like his stepfather but never made a success of either. He died of tuberculosis at age thirty-four and left a mountain of debts that his stepfather had to pay off and two children. Florence didn't want to have anything to do with them as she had wanted nothing to do with her own son.

Personal Notes: Tall, gawky, and headstrong, Florence was described as having a very masculine manner. She wore her hair marceled (in waves made with a curling iron) and, instead of glasses, a pince-nez (eyeglasses clipped to the nose). She did not like to have her photograph taken and if pressed by photographers, would only pose in profile. In addition to her music, she loved to roller skate, ride horseback, and was fond of Beeman's pepsin chewing gum. Florence had two pet canaries, Pete and Bob. When she left the White House, she gave Bob to Maggie Rogers, a White House maid who was popularized by daughter Lillian in the book, *Backstairs at the White House.* She was a firm believer in "the stars" and often consulted medium Madame Marcia with her good friend, Evalyn Walsh MacLean. Marcia consulted Harding's birth date and told Florence her senator husband would become president.

Politician's Wife: Florence was a driving, "nagging" force in Harding's career, both in the private and public sectors. She was more ambitious for him than he was. In order to protect him from what she considered evil influences, she followed him everywhere. She went to work at his Marion *Star* newspaper for a few days and stayed fourteen years. While there, she had the reputation of being a penny pincher. She encouraged Harding to run for office, supervised the spending of campaign funds, fought with campaign chairman Harry Daugherty, and organized his schedule. When he played poker with his cronies, she went along and tended bar. She was stricken with a near fatal kidney ailment, which resulted in the removal of one kidney in 1905. Harding, for the first time in their marriage, was free to travel and do what he wanted.

When Harding was elected U.S. senator, he and Florence bought a home at 2314 Wyoming Avenue in Washington, D.C. During World

War I, Florence often visited injured soldiers at Walter Reed Army Hospital. She always wore the same hat "so the boys will know I'm here." Jealous, suspicious, and vindictive, Florence kept a little red book that listed Harding's and "her" enemies.

First Lady: The Hardings brought midwestern folksiness to the White House. Harding gave his wife a diamond sunburst pin as an inaugural gift. She placed the pin on a black velvet band that she wore around her neck like a collar. The collar, which she wore constantly to hid wrinkles, became her trademark. She gave large garden parties and loved to mingle with guests. Garden clubs named several varieties of sweet peas and roses after her. Her favorite shade of blue was nicknamed "Harding Blue." Florence enjoyed joining tours that visited the White House. She pointed out artifacts and stood for hours shaking hands with anyone who approached her. When the Girl Scouts visited, she wore one of their uniforms; when veterans came, she wore her familiar old hat. In 1922, she was again stricken with kidney problems. When Harding decided to take a transcontinental trip in the summer of 1923, Florence invited herself along. On the return from Alaska, Harding fell ill and died in San Francisco. Mysterious circumstances surround his death and some, including Gaston Means, a former investigator for the Department of Justice and a convicted perjurer, have claimed that Florence poisoned him. Means claimed she was tired of Harding's philandering ways (with Nan Britton and Carrie Phillips) and that she wanted to spare him the scandal of Teapot Dome. To compound the mystery, Florence refused to allow an autopsy to be performed and, six months later, Harding's personal physician, Dr. Charles Sawyer, also died. Again, the only one with him when he died was Florence. Florence herself died in 1924, without answering any questions about their deaths.

Death: One month before dying of kidney disease at age sixty-four, Florence had a premonition of her own death. Rev. Dr. Jesse Swank conducted the Methodist memorial service assisted by Baptist pastor Rev. Dr. George Ladis. The Columbus (Ohio) Glee Club sang her favorite songs including "The End of a Perfect Day," and the 10th U.S. Infantry served as honor guard. Burial was in Marion Cemetery, at the Harding Memorial. The Hardings are the second presidential couple to both die before his four-year term was up.

GRACE ANNA GOODHUE COOLIDGE

(1879–1957)

First Lady (1923–1929)

The Straight Facts

Born: January 3, 1879
Birthplace: Burlington, Vermont
Ancestry: English
Physical Characteristics: 5'4" tall, brown hair, green-gray eyes
Religion: Congregationalist
Husband: Calvin Coolidge (1872–1933)
Date of Marriage: October 4, 1905
Place of Marriage: Burlington, Vermont

Children: Two sons
Died: July 8, 1957
Place of Death: Northhampton, Massachusetts
Burial Place: Plymouth Notch Cemetery, Plymouth Notch, Vermont
Firsts: To be born in Vermont
Incumbent First Lady to vote for her husband as President
To receive an honorary college degree
To serve as president of a national sorority
White House Portrait: Howard Chandler Christy, China Room

The More Colorful Facts

Astrological Sign: Capricorn
Nicknames: Mammy, Cal's Safety Valve, First Lady of Baseball
Childhood and Family Life: Grace was the daughter of mechanical engineer
turned steamboat inspector Andrew Isaachar Goodhue and Lemira
Barrett. Grace was born at their home on Shelburne and St. Paul
Streets in Burlington, Vermont. The Goodhues moved to a larger
home on Maple Street when Grace was three. As a child she had trouble with her spine and suffered from sinusitis. She attended Burlington
High School (Class of 1897), the University of Vermont, and wor-
shiped at the College Street Congregational Church. A founding member of the Beta chapter of Pi Beta Phi sorority, many meetings were
held in the Goodhue home. Graduating with a Ph.B. degree in 1902
from college, she joined family friend Dr. Caroline A. Yale as a teacher
at the Clarke Institute for the Deaf in Northampton, Massachusetts.
Courtship and Marriage: While watering flowers in front of Baker Hill, the
Clarke teachers' residence, Grace saw a man in a neighboring building
shaving, dressed only in a union suit and straw hat. It was Calvin Coolidge. He heard her laugh, liked what he saw, and asked for an introduction. He explained the hat was to control a stubborn cowlick.
Courting was done by walking about town, picnicking, and visiting
nearby Mt. Tom. His first gift to her was a porcelain replica of the
mountain. Coolidge went to Burlington to talk to Capt. Goodhue:

> "Up here on some law business, Mr. Coolidge?"
> "No. Up here to ask your permission to marry Grace."
> "Does she know it?"
> "No, but she soon will."

The Goodhues wanted them to wait a year so Grace could learn
to be a wife and how to bake bread. Coolidge wouldn't wait, saying he
could buy bread. They were wed in the Goodhue home by the Rev. Ed-

ward Hungerford, with Miss Ethel Stevens and Dr. A. H. McCormick as witnesses. Grace wore a gray gown with velvet bows and carried autumn flowers. There were no attendants and only fifteen guests. A two-week honeymoon to Montreal was cut short because Coolidge had to return to Northampton to campaign for the school board, a sign of things to come. Grace didn't even know he was running. Shortly after their marriage, the thirty-three-year-old groom presented his twenty-six-year-old bride with fifty-two pairs of socks that needed to be mended. Grace was not a very good cook; Coolidge liked to drop her biscuits on the floor, then stamp his feet, insinuating how hard they were. Coolidge enjoyed picking out her clothes and the frugal New Englander spared no expense when it came to her. He set their schedules and if he felt she was staying out too late with her friends, he would call and tell her to come home.

Children: The Coolidges had two sons. John (1906-) married the daughter of the governor of Connecticut in 1929 and became a successful businessman. Calvin, Jr. (1908–1924) died of blood poisoning. After playing tennis without socks, he developed a blister on his heel which turned septic. Both parents were devasted by his death. Coolidge often said ". . . . with him went the power and the glory of the presidency." After his death, the White House staff would place a single white rose in a bud vase in front of his picture each day, even when the Coolidges were not in residence. A Vermont spruce was planted on the White House lawn in his honor.

Personal Notes: Grace was an avid reader, smoked cigarettes, played the piano, and sang contralto in a glee club. She liked to walk in the woods, ice skate, to garden, and enjoyed music and the theatre. Grace's favorite card games were gin rummy, hilo jack, and 500 rummy. She liked pink or yellow roses, gardenias, and wildflowers, especially gumbolilies and shooting stars. Her favorite color was pink, her best-loved hymn "Holy Spirit Truth Divine."

Grace also loved animals and kept a large menagerie at the White House, including white collies Rob Roy (formerly Oshkosh) and Prudence Prim (always dressed in a hat); chow Tiny Tim; raccoon Rebecca; airedale Paul Pry (formerly Laddie Buck); red shetland Diana of Wildwood (renamed Calamity Jane, then Jolly Jane); Hartz mountain canaries Nip and Tuck; white canary Snowflake; and thrush Old Bill. She enjoyed baseball; her favorite team was the Boston Red Sox and later the Washington Senators. Her good-luck charm was an ivory elephant, the symbol of the Republican Party.

Politician's Wife: Grace stayed in Northampton to raise the boys and care for their duplex at 21 Massasoit Street. Governor Coolidge lived in the Adams Hotel in Boston, renting two rooms for family visits. Grace did not get involved much with politics and Coolidge rarely shared his plans and policies with her; they did little entertaining. She told reporters, "Mr. Coolidge may be governor of Massachusetts, but I am first of all mother to my boys." She served on the board of Mercersburg Academy for twelve years, was a trustee of Clarke School, was a national president of Pi Beta Phi in 1915, and was involved with Edwards Congregational Church (named for Puritan Jonathan Edwards). During World War I she was active in the Red Cross.

First Lady: Charming, vivacious, outgoing Grace was a change from both her predecessor and her quiet husband. She was called Coolidge's greatest asset because of her warm, giving ways. Forbidden by Coolidge to speak in public, she once answered reporters in sign language for the deaf. Coolidge continued to set her schedule and wouldn't let her fly in a plane, bob her hair, wear short skirts, or ride a horse. The White House staff called her Sunshine. After Cal, Jr.'s death, they did little entertaining. While the White House was being repaired, they lived at DuPont Circle

Death: At the age of seventy-eight she died of heart disease at Road Fork, her Northampton home. She is buried next to her husband and youngest son in Plymouth Notch.

LOU HENRY HOOVER
(1875–1944)
First Lady (1929–1933)

The Straight Facts

Born: March 29, 1875
Birthplace: Waterloo, Iowa
Ancestry: English
Physical Characteristics: 5'8" tall, brown hair, blue eyes
Religion: Episcopalian, later Quaker
Husband: Herbert Clark Hoover (1841–1964)
Date of Marriage: February 10, 1899
Place of Marriage: Monterey, California
Children: Two sons
Died: January 7, 1944

Place of Death: New York, New York
Burial Place: Hoover Presidential Library, West Branch, Iowa
Firsts: To be born in Iowa
> To deliver a speech on radio
White House Portrait: Richard M. Brown, after Philip de Laszlo, East Wing Reception Room

The More Colorful Facts

Astrological Sign: Aries
Nickname: Mother
Childhood and Family Life: Lou was the oldest of two daughters of banker Charles Delano Henry and Florence Ida (de) Weed. Her paternal great-grandfather helped lay out the town of Wooster, Ohio. As a child Lou was often seen romping in the woods with her curly-haired bird dog Logan. She was a good athlete who excelled in baseball, skating, basketball, and archery. Her father took her hunting, camping, and fishing. When her father developed a bronchial condition, the family moved to California, first to Whittier, and then to Monterey. Lou attended Waterloo Grade School (editor of the school newspaper, *Boomerang*), State Normal School in Los Angeles (class president), San Jose Normal School (Class of 1894), and Stanford University (BA, 1898). She received a teaching certificate at San Jose but returned to school to study geology, the only girl in the class.
Courtship and Marriage: Professor John Caspar Brannar introduced freshman Lou to his prized pupil, senior Herbert Hoover. They began dating and he was often to be found in front of Robel Hall where she lived or at Kappa Kappa Gamma dances. Lou and Hoover had an "understanding" when he graduated and went to Australia to mine for gold. Soon after Lou graduated from Stanford, Hoover was appointed chief engineer for the Chinese Engineering and Mining Company. He proposed by wire and she accepted by cablegram. They were to be married before he left for the Orient. Hoover was a Quaker and Lou an Episcopalian and no minister of either faith lived in Monterey. The local justice of the peace was family friend Fr. Ramon Mestres, a Catholic priest. The twenty-three-year-old bride and her groom were married by Fr. Mestres in the parlor of the Henry home. After a one-night honeymoon in San Francisco, they sailed to China.
Children: The Hoovers had two sons. Herbert Charles (1903–1969) was a geophysicist and an under-secretary of state. Allan Henry (1907–) is a retired businessman.

Personal Notes: She could speak five languages and was a good knitter. Her favorite colors were brown and beige. She collected fine Chinese white-and-blue porcelain, especially vases of the K'ang Hse and Ming periods. She was also very superstitious.

Engineers's Wife: When the Hoovers reached Tientsin, China, they set up a household and worked together to seek minerals. No matter where they lived, the first picture hung in their home was a lithograph of Abraham Lincoln signing the Emancipation Proclamation. Lou became fluent in Chinese and translated materials for Hoover and gave instructions to workers. In 1900, the Hoovers became caught in the middle of the Boxer Rebellion. Lou was cool and courageous under fire, helped tend the wounded, distributed food, and made daily observation rounds on her bicycle. She was quite amused to read a three-column obituary of herself in a Peking newspaper after the fighting had stopped.

In 1897, they went to London, where Hoover became a junior partner in Bewick, Moreing, and Company. For the next thirteen years they traveled all over the globe. By the time Herbert, Jr. was one year old, he had been around the world twice. In 1912, Lou translated, in both of their names, *Agricola's De Re Metallic,* written by German George Beura in Latin in 1556. For this comprehensive work, she won the Mining and Metallurgical Award. She also helped her husband write his classic *Principles of Mining.* In 1908, a senior partner of Bewick, Moreing embezzled corporate funds. Hoover drew up the plans to pay back the creditors. Lou paid the wife and four children of the embezzler an allowance while he was in jail. After paying off all the debts, Hoover left to form his own firm.

Politician's Wife: The start of World War I saw the Hoovers living in London at their Kensington Gardens home nicknamed "The Red House." During the aerial bombing of London, they found their two young sons watching from the roof. Lou decided it was time they went to school in America. Lou and her sons sailed on the SS *Lusitania,* just eight months before she was sunk. Returning to London, both Lou and Hoover were involved in the war relief effort.

Lou served as president of the Society of American Women in London, was on the executive committee of the American Women's War Relief Fund and Hospital, and organized the California chapter of the Committee of Mercy. She volunteered for Red Cross duty and opened her home to American servicemen and travelers caught abroad. She also helped establish the Women's Hospital in Belgium.

Returning to America, she continued to support war relief efforts. She also became involved with the Girl Scouts, serving as leader of Troop 7 and later serving as national president. She was nicknamed Buffalo by her charges as she encouraged physical exercise, especially swimming. In 1922, she was the only female officer of the National Amateur Athletic Federation.

When Hoover was appointed secretary of commerce by President Warren Harding, they moved to 2300 S Street in Washington. Meal times at the Hoover home were always filled with guests as they enjoyed lively conversations and discussions. For many years, she played Mrs. Santa Claus at the Children's Hospital in the nation's capital.

First Lady: Lou used her experience as a diplomatic wife to make the White House stylish and entertaining. She restored the Monroe Room and catalogued the artwork. Dinners were lavish affairs with as many as seven courses. They continued their practice of inviting interesting people to meals. A senator might find himself sitting with a Girl Scout and a society matron with a college student. As First Lady, Lou's first White House reception was for 1,800 guests. She rarely wore jewels, never wore high heels, did her own hair, and drove herself around Washington. She also drew much criticism for inviting Mrs. Oscar De-Priest, the wife of a black congressman from Chicago, to a congressional tea at the White House.

Lou supervised the plans for a summer retreat, Rapidan, in the Blue Ridge Mountains. When the Hoovers left the White House, this home was turned over to the government for use by the Girl and Boy Scouts. Her mascot became "Billy," a possum she caught on the White House lawn. Billy was often chased by dogs Pat and Weegie.

She abolished two White House customs that had plagued First Ladies for over 150 years. The annual New Year's Day reception was abolished because it was so unmanageable. She also eliminated the custom of receiving and returning calls.

Used to servants, the Hoovers relationship with the White House staff was somewhat strange. Lou communicated orders through hand signals. Servants were not allowed to use elevators or be seen by guests, with the exception of those servants in livery. Most peculiar was Lou's custom of leaving a $1,000 bill on the top of her bureau. (If she was testing the servants' honesty, she would have had better luck with smaller denominations. No one misses $1; everyone misses $1,000.)

Post White House: The Hoovers returned to Palo Alto, California, near the Stanford University campus. Lou designed their home, Hopi Indian style, on a hill overlooking the campus. She continued to be active in the Girl Scouts, the Community Chest, women's groups, the League of Women Voters, the Visiting Nurses Association, and the YMCA. In · 1940, she served as president of the Western Women's Committee.

Death: The Hoovers visited New York City in January 1944, and one afternoon Lou attended a concert. That evening, she suffered a heart attack, and died suddenly at age sixty-eight in the Waldorf Astoria Hotel. Her funeral, conducted by Rev. Dr. George P. Sargent of St. Bartholomew's Church, was attended by hundreds of mourners. Her favorite hymn, "Nearer, My God To Thee," was played. She was buried at Alta Mesa Cemetery in Palo Alto, but was reinterred at at the Hoover Presidential Library in 1964.

Honors/Honorary Degrees

Cross of Chevalier, Order of Leopold (Belgium), 1915
Mills College, 1923
Whittier College, 1928
Swarthmore College. 1929
Elmira College. 1930
Goucher College, 1931
College of Wooster, 1932
Tufts University, 1932
Stanford University, 1941

Buildings

Lou Henry Hoover Memorial YMCA Building, Palo Alto
Lou Henry Hoover Building, Stanford University campus

ANNA ELEANOR ROOSEVELT
(1884–1962)
First Lady (1933–1945)

The Straight Facts

Born: October 11, 1884
Birthplace: New York, New York
Ancestry: Dutch, English
Physical Characteristics: 5'9" tall, golden-blonde hair, blue eyes
Religion: Presbyterian
Husband: Franklin Delano Roosevelt (1882–1945)
Date of Marriage: March 17, 1905
Place of Marriage: New York, New York
Children: Five sons, one daughter
Death: November 7, 1962
Place of Death: New York, New York
Burial Place: Hyde Park, New York

Firsts: To give a formal press conference
To ride in an airplane
To testify before a senate committee
To serve as ambassador to the United Nations
White House Portrait: Douglas Chandor*, Vermeil Room

The More Colorful Facts

Astrological Sign: Libra
Nickname: Babs, Granny, Little Nell, Totty, First Lady of the World, Assistant President, That Old Hoot Owl, Great Gabbo, World's Most Admired Woman, Hatchet Face, La Boca Grande, My Missus
Childhood and Family Life: Eleanor was the only daughter of Elliott Roosevelt and his fashionable wife, Anna Livingston Hall. One of her mother's ancestors, Robert R. Livingston, was the judge who delivered the oath of office to George Washington as first president of the United States. Three other Livingston relatives signed the Declaration of Independence. Both families were well-to-do and Eleanor's parents were considered two of Society's "beautiful people." Elliott suffered from a brain tumor and turned to drink to ease his pain.

Eleanor was a shy, awkward, old-fashioned child. She was deeply hurt when her mother called her Granny; her father called her Little Nell, from a character in Charles Dicken's *Old Curiosity Shop*. She was full of childhood phobias including fear of the dark, horses, snakes, dogs, and other children. She suffered from a spinal defect and was forced to wear a back brace. Both parents died before she was ten years old. Eleanor and her two younger brothers went to live with their grandmother, Mary Livingston Ludlow Hall. Grandmother Hall took her responsibility seriously but without love. Eleanor was forced to wear clothes that were both old-fashioned and not appropriate for her age, attend school at home with tutors, and was not given an opportunity to meet children her own age. Her life changed for the better at age fifteen when she was sent for three years to Allenswood, the spartan English finishing school outside London.

Allenswood's headmistress, Mlle. Marie Souvestre gave Eleanor the first real love and understanding she had ever known. Under Mlle. Souvestre's tutelage, Eleanor advanced her education, learned to dress

* The Roosevelt family had hired Chandor for $2,000 to paint the portrait which took twelve sittings to complete. When it was finished, Chandor demanded $10,000 and the family declined acceptance. Lady Bird Johnson bought the portrait from Chandor's widow during her tenure.

properly, and developed poise and confidence in her abilities. These were the happiest years of her young life.

Courtship and Marriage: Returning to New York after graduation, Eleanor taught calisthenics and dancing at the Rivington Street Settlement House. She also joined the fledgling Junior League and the Consumers League. Eleanor made her debut at the Academy Society Ball. She attended all the debutante parties and was presented at numerous cotillions and balls. Eleanor didn't enjoy the fuss and did not think she was a good dancer or socializer. One person who did notice her was fifth cousin Franklin Delano Roosevelt, who had journeyed from Harvard to attend the parties.

Franklin was her father's godson and remembered playing "horsey" with Eleanor when she was a baby. They enjoyed long talks together and soon were dating regularly. She was quite shocked when, one year later, he proposed. He was handsome, a man-about-town, and Eleanor still thought of herself as plain and uninteresting. However, she accepted his proposal. Then they had to face FDR's mother, the formidable Sara (known to Eleanor as Cousin Sally).

Sara Delano had big plans for her son, which did not include a "mouse" of a wife like Eleanor. She quickly arranged a trip to the Caribbean for her son in the hopes that he would change his mind. He didn't, and the engagement was formally announced in November of 1904. The marriage was to take place in the spring when Eleanor's Uncle Ted, President Theodore Roosevelt, could arrange his schedule to give the bride away.

The wedding took place at the adjoining 76th Street homes of Eleanor's aunts, Mrs. Henry (Susie) Parish and Mrs. E. Livingston Ludlow. The connecting parlor doors were opened to accommodate all the guests. The twenty-year-old bride wore a satin wedding gown covered with rose point Brussels lace and carried a bouquet of lillies of the valley. Eleanor paid tribute to her long-dead mother by wearing Anna's diamond brooch to secure the veil and marrying on Anna's birthday. Cousin Alice Roosevelt served as maid of honor. Lathrup Brown served as best man and the Rev. Dr. Endicott Peabody of Groton officiated. After the ceremony, the bridal couple was nearly neglected as most guests crowded around the president. They took a brief honeymoon at Hyde Park, and when FDR returned to Columbia Law School, they lived at the Hotel Webster. At summer's break, they took a long honeymoon in Europe and returned to the New York City home Sara bought fo them at the Draper House, which FDR called his fourteen-foot mansion.

Children: The Roosevelts had six children. Anna, named after her mother and grandmother (1906–1975), was married three times. During World War II she and her two children lived at the White House. James (1907–), who has also been married three times, was a member of Congress and is currently a financial consultant. Before he was born, the Roosevelts thought they were expecting twins. Elliott (1910–) has been married four times, served as mayor of Miami Beach, and is the author of numerous murder mystery novels featuring his mother. Franklin, Jr. (1914–1988) was married three times and also served in Congress. John (1916–1982) was married twice and was a stockbroker. The first Franklin, Jr. lived only seven months.

Personal Notes: Eleanor was very superstitious; she never seated thirteen for a meal. She spoke French from the age of two and Spanish. She loved to knit and was always working with her hands. She preferred writing letters to using the telephone. Her favorite flower was the rose, and she liked strawberry jam.

She believed in exercising every morning to control her "pot." She took a variety of vitamin pills, including garlic tablets, to improve her memory. After exercise, she would take a long cold shower. She preferred lemon juice instead of orange juice for breakfast. Every afternoon, after a one-hour walk, she would take tea. When the weather permitted, she swam in the pool. She had been taught to swim by Uncle Ted who believed in throwing the children in the water so they would learn how to swim. From then on, she never put her face underwater without holding her nose. Her fear of water developed at age three when a ship carrying Eleanor and her parents to Europe sank and little Eleanor ended up in one of the HMS *Britannic's* lifeboats.

She learned to ride the same way she learned to swim. Eleanor kept her horse, Dot, at Fort Myers and rode in Rock Creek Park. She had bought Dot from trooper Earl Miller whom she had befriended in Albany. As with most of her friends, he was the recipient of numerous letters from her. When Miller's third wife sued for divorce, she found the letters and named Eleanor codefendent in the divorce proceedings. When it was proved that Eleanor had written letters to hundreds of people, her part of the suit was dropped.

Politician's Wife: Upon FDR's graduation from law school, the family moved to another home bought for them by Sara, an adjoining brownstone on E. 65th Street, similar to Aunt Susie's 76th-Street house. Again Sara hired the servants, the nursemaids, and decorated the house to her taste and not Eleanor's. When FDR was elected to the state Senate, they moved to Albany and, for once, Eleanor was out from under Sara's thumb. At the time, Eleanor had little interest in politics and was surprised to hear FDR's views on women's rights. She began attending legislative sessions and learning how government works.

In 1913, they moved to Washington when FDR was appointed assistant secretary of the navy. They lived at 1733 N Street. Auntie Bye (Anna Roosevelt Cowles) taught Eleanor the social protocol in Washington. During World War I, she knit for the Red Cross and volunteered at canteens for soldiers. She became interested in the suffrage movement, supported the League of Nations, and joined the League of Women Voters. After the 1920 election, which saw FDR as the Democratic vice-presidential candidate, they returned to New York and their old home. She also took political "lessons" from FDR's friend and advisor, Louis Howe.

Two traumatic personal events happened during this time that were to shape the Eleanor the world now knows. First was her discovery that FDR had been having an affair with her social secretary, Lucy Page Mercer. Eleanor offered to divorce him, but it was decided that for the children and his political career, this would be unwise. FDR promised not to see Lucy again and Eleanor moved into a separate bedroom. She also decided to pursue her own interests and not be subservient to his ideas and activities. The other was when FDR contracted polio in 1921. In order to keep FDR abreast of what was happening in the state, Eleanor became his eyes, ears, and legs. She told him "I'm only being active [sic] till you can be again."

When FDR was elected governor of New York, Eleanor continued to be involved with social causes. She taught at Todhunter School and developed a furniture factory at Val-Kill, her cottage on the Hyde Park grounds. She became involved with newspapers at this time and edited the *Women's Democratic News*. Because FDR couldn't walk, she visited hospitals, state homes, jails, and schools. When he didn't heed her advice, she would invite someone to dinner who held the same view as she did, and together they would try to persuade him to change his mind. She was not in favor of his entering the presidential race in 1932, but campaigned hard for his election.

First Lady: Before the 1933 inauguration, Lou Hoover invited Eleanor to tour the White House and offered to send a limousine and escort. Eleanor said that she preferred to walk. The staff soon learned this was a different type of First Lady. She wanted to run the elevator by herself and even helped move furniture.

A self-admitted bad cook, Eleanor claimed only to know how to cook hot dogs and scrambled eggs, which were served every Sunday evening. However, Eleanor only cooked the eggs; the staff had prepared the mixture. When the king and queen of England were served hot dogs at Hyde Park, that was all they got. There were no buns, no condiments, and no baked beans. To Eleanor, food was something only to sustain the body. She did not plan menus, leaving that to head housekeeper Henriette Nesbitt.

The Roosevelts had a large, extended family living in the White House. In addition to their children, various grandchildren, FDR's mother, and Louis Howe, they invited numerous other friends to stay with them. FDR's assistant, Missy Le Hand, lived on the third floor; advisor Harry Hopkins and his motherless daughter, Diana, lived on the second floor. To Eleanor, they were just one big noisy, happy family. She tried to hang a swing from one of the White House trees for the children, but superintendent of buildings, Ulysses S. Grant III, would not allow her to deface public property. (Forty years later, President Jimmy Carter would build a tree house for daughter Amy in one of these trees, apparently causing little damage.)

When FDR initiated his "Alphabet Soup" social programs, Eleanor traveled around the country reporting her findings to him. She also had her own special projects, such as Arthurdale in West Virginia. It was a self-sustaining homestead community. She also helped develop the National Youth Administration, and FDR selected a young Texan named Lyndon B. Johnson to head it. In addition to improving the plight of women, the homeless, and the disabled, she advocated better conditions for blacks.

In a famous political and social incident, Eleanor resigned her membership in the Daughters of the American Revolution (DAR) over their refusal to allow black singer Marian Anderson to perform at their Constitution Hall. According to the DAR, they did refuse permission, but only for the day Miss Anderson wanted to appear, as the hall was already booked. Eleanor later showed her support for Miss Anderson by inviting her to sing for the king and queen of England.

She also wrote a number of newspaper columns; the most famous was "My Day," which she began writing in 1935 and continued until her death. She also had her own radio show and gave speeches.

During World War II, FBI chief J. Edgar Hoover dubbed her "Rover" because she traveled so much. Because FDR couldn't, she visited the battlefront (in a Red Cross Uniform), ate with soldiers in their mess halls, and spent countless hours in hospital wards. She would call families or write them when she returned home. She flew around the world twice and logged more than 500,000 miles. Eleanor loved to fly and once contemplated taking flying lessons from Amelia Earhart, but FDR convinced her it was a waste of time as she couldn't afford her own plane.

She was not in favor of FDR's running for a third term; she thought it would be bad for his health. War was declared less than a year after he was inaugurated for the third time. When he ran for a fourth term she knew, in her heart, he would not survive.

"What a boon for the Hotel Business" was the caption for this Dorman H. Smith political cartoon referring to Eleanor Roosevelt's penchant for globe-trotting.

Eleanor was speaking at the Sulgrave Club when she was summoned back to the White House and told that FDR was dead. It was she who broke the news to Vice-President Harry Truman. While on the way to Warm Springs to pick up the president's body, she learned that Lucy Mercer, now Mrs. Winthrup Rutherfurd, had been with FDR when he died. Upon leaving Washington, she said that chapter of her life was closed and went into seclusion at Val-Kill.

Post White House: Eleanor's seclusion did not last for long. She quickly resumed her writing, teaching, and causes. She was elected to the boards of the Americans for Democratic Action, the National Association for the Advancement of Colored People, and the American delegation to the fledgling United Nations. As UN delegate, she was instrumental in getting the Human Rights Amendment passed. She continued traveling, usually with her good friend, Lorena Hickock. Some have claimed their's was an immoral relationship.

She again served the UN when John Kennedy became president. She arrived for the 1960 inauguration on a train from New York, unannounced, carrying her own bag. She refused his invitation to sit on the platform with him because she could not stand his father, Joe Kennedy.

In her later years, Eleanor's health began to fail. A car accident in 1946 resulted in the loss of two front teeth. She had a bridge put in and enjoyed her new straight teeth. Her driver's license was also suspended for four months. She wore glasses constantly and had a hearing aid installed. She started losing her hair and wore hair nets or wigs to keep the remaining strands in place.

In 1960, it was discovered she had aplastic anemia (tuberculosis of the bone marrow), and she received frequent blood transfusions. Neither the country nor her children were told her true condition. She developed phlebitis and could not walk for several weeks until the swelling receded.

Death: Eleanor died at age seventy-eight of aplastic anemia in her New York apartment. She had made her own funeral arrangements, requesting a simple oak coffin and, in lieu of flowers, a bough of evergreens from her beloved Val-Kill, where she wished to be buried in the garden. A simple stone was to mark the spot with only her name and years of birth and death. No reference was to be made of her serving as First Lady. She chose her own pallbearers (including the owner of the Hyde Park Luncheonette), and she wanted a simple service. The latter was impossible to fulfill. Guests were given different colored invitations depending on their relationship to her or rank. The Roosevelt children had to wear passes with their pictures on them to avoid being swallowed up in the crowd. There were two memorial services, in New York and Washington. Adlai Stevenson delivered the eulogy.

Honors/Honorary Degrees

American Peace Award, 1923
First Annual Franklin D. Roosevelt Brotherhood Award, 1946
First American Award in Human Relations. 1949
Four Freedoms Medal, 1950
Prince Carl Medal (Sweden), 1950
Irving Geist Foundation, 1950
National Society for Crippled Children and Adults, 1950
Nansen Medal, 1954
Medal of Honor for Visual Arts, 1959
Murray Green-Meany Award, 1955
Brandeis University, 1957

Publications

When You Grow Up to Vote, 1932
Hunting Big Game in the Eighties (editor), 1932
It's Up to the Women, 1933
A Trip to Washington with Bobby and Betty, 1937
This Is My Story, 1937
My Days, 1938
Christmas, a story by Eleanor Roosevelt, 1940
The Moral Basis of Democracy (editor), 1940
If You Ask Me, 1946
This I Remember, 1949
India, the Awakening East, 1952
On My Own, 1958
You Learn By Living, 1960
The Autobiography of Eleanor Roosevelt, 1961

ELIZABETH VIRGINIA WALLACE TRUMAN

(1885–1982)

First Lady (1945–1953)

The Straight Facts

Born: February 13, 1885
Birthplace: Independence, Missouri
Ancestry: English
Physical Characteristics: 5'4" tall, 140 lbs., blonde hair, blue eyes
Religion: Presbyterian, then Episcopalian
Husband: Harry S Truman (1884–1972)
Date of Marriage: June 28, 1919
Place of Marriage: Independence, Missouri
Children: One daughter
Died: October 18, 1982
Place of Death: Independence, Missouri
Burial Place: Harry S Truman Library & Museum, Independence, Missouri
Firsts: To install air conditioning in the White House
White House Portrait: Martha Greta Kempton, East Wing Lobby

The More Colorful Facts

Astrological Sign: Aquarius

Nicknames: Bess, The Boss, Independent Lady from Independence, Housewife #1, Two-Gun Bess, Payroll Bess

Childhood and Family Life: Bess was the oldest of five children born to merchant/politican David Willock Wallace and Margaret Elizabeth (Madge) Gates. She was named after a friend of her mother's, Bessie Madge Andrews, and Paternal grandmother Virginia Willock Wallace. Outgoing and athletic, she attended local schools and Miss Barlow's (finishing) School in Kansas City.

Courtship and Marriage: Five-year-old Bess met six-year-old Harry S Truman in a Sunday School class at the First Prebyterian Church. The Trumans were Baptists, but there was no Baptist church in Independence at that time. Truman claimed it was love at first sight. They became friends in the fifth grade but shy bookworm Truman was no competition for the extroverted, athletic Bess. They both went to Independence High but never dated. After graduation, Truman went to work in Kansas City and only visited Independence on weekends. One day, he was asked to return a plate to the Wallace house, and he ran the whole way.

They had their first date in 1910, and he regularly took the one-hour train ride to visit her. He also began what was to become a lifelong tradition with them, writing letters when they were apart from each other. In one 1911 letter he proposed but she turned him down. In 1913, they had an "understanding" and in 1917 were formally engaged. The marriage was held up while Truman served in World War I, and he carried her picture with him to France.

Upon his return, thirty-five-year-old Major Harry Truman married his 34-year-old sweetheart. They were married by the Rev. Dr. John V. Plunkett at Trinity Episcopal Church in Independence. The bride wore a white georgette dress with three-quarter-length belle sleeves and white buckled kid slippers. She also wore a wide-brimmed hat of white faille and carried a prayer book and Aaron roses. She was attended by cousins Louise Wells and Helen Wallace and given away by brother Frank Wallace. Ted Marks served as best man. They honeymooned in Chicago and Port Huron, Michigan. Returning to Independence, they lived in the Wallace home.

Children: After several miscarriages, Bess gave birth to her only child, Mary Margaret, in 1924. After college graduation, "Margie," as she was called, embarked on a singing career with mixed success. She married newsman E. Clifton Daniels and they have four sons. She has become a successful journalist and has written biographies of her parents and several mystery novels, all set in Washington, D.C.

Personal Notes: Bess was a good athlete who was described as the best shot-putter in Independence. As a child she also excelled at tennis, horseback riding, fishing, and played a mean third base. Her favorite color was blue. She liked yellow roses, red tulips, and azaleas. She knitted, enjoyed detective novels, and was an avid bridge player. Bess was fond of chocolate carmel sundaes and angel food cake. Her favorite movies were the "Road" pictures with Bing Crosby, Bob Hope, and Dorothy Lamour. She was a member of Chapter S of the Pi Epsilon Omega sorority. And, like her husband, she preferred her old-fashioned cocktails strong.

Politician's Wife: After the Truman & Jacobsen's Haberdashery went bankrupt in 1922, Truman ran for a local judgeship. While Bess had worked beside him in the store, even keeping the books, she would not be an active participant in the political game. Fiercely protective of her privacy, she stayed at home running the household, which now included Margaret and numerous other Gates-Wallace relatives. She made no appearances for him, very few with him, and refused to deliver a speech.

Reluctantly, Bess became drawn into his run for the Senate. She worked at campaign headquarters, read his speeches, and gave advice. Truman called her a shrewd judge of character and very intuitive. After his election, he went to Washington alone, found an apartment, and begged her to come with him. She agreed to spend one-half of the year in Washington and the other half in Independence. They later moved to a larger apartment at 4700 Connecticut Ave. When in Washington, Bess worked in his office opening mail, escorting constituents around town, typing letters, and doing research. For this, she was put on the payroll at $4,500 per year. It was a common practice for congressional members to place family members who worked in their offices on the payroll. However, Clare Booth Luce accused them of wrongdoing and leaked stories to the press of "Payroll Bess." Truman sent Luce a blistering letter telling her she could insult him but not Bess and that his wife earned every penny of her salary.

Bess was not happy with the cleaning services in Washington and sent their laundry to Kansas City by mail to be cleaned.

During World War II, Bess, a member of the Senate Wives Club, worked at the Red Cross and rolled bandages. She was proud but not happy when Truman was elected vice-president in 1944. She didn't like the fishbowl they would now be living in. Her Secret Service name while "Second Lady" was Fern-Lake; she didn't like being followed everywhere she went. She stopped going to the Senate Wives Club because, as the vice-president's wife, she would now be the president of the group.

First Lady: Bess and Margaret were at home when Truman called to tell them that President Franklin Roosevelt had died. Bess' first official act as First Lady was to console Eleanor Roosevelt and tell her she could stay at the White House as long as necessary. Then, Bess watched her husband sworn in as thirty-third president. Reporters were shocked to discover that on her first full day as First Lady, Bess made breakfast, made the bed, washed dishes, dusted, vaccuumed, and then read a detective novel, *The Crimson Claw.* They were soon to find out this was a different sort of First Lady.

Unlike her predecessor, she would give no press conferences and usually responded to any questions with a terse "no comment." She said she had no opinions on public policy because she had never been elected to anything, so no one should be interested in anything she had to say. She did hold informal teas for reporters but with the understanding that anything she said was off the record. As before, she was her husband's full partner and best advisor. She also tried to curb his salty, blunt language. When one society matron complained that he had used the word "manure" in public, Bess replied that it had taken her twenty years to get him to say manure.

Bess ran the household, oversaw expenditures, clipped coupons, shopped, and drove herself around Washington. For a while, both of the Trumans' mothers lived in the White House with them. She addressed her own Christmas cards and entertained members of the Tuesday Bridge Club to a four-day tour of Washington and the "Great White Jail," as she called the White House. Head housekeeper Henrietta Nesbitt left after refusing Bess a stick of butter to take to a bridge game.

The Truman family was very happy in one another's company. The White House staff dubbed them the "Three Musketeers." Bess was usually right in the middle of any escapades and her infectious laugh was often heard. The Secret Service dubbed her "Sunshine." Amusing stories have been told of watermelon seed fights, heated Ping-Pong games, and broken bed slats in the presidential bedroom.

Bess reluctantly agreed to accompany Truman on his 1948 whistlestop campaign. No paper gave him a chance of winning, but the Trumans gamely traveled on. At each stop, Truman would make a speech and then introduce Bess as "The Boss" and Margaret as "The One Who Bosses the Boss." He stopped only after both threatened to leave the train if he did it one more time. On election night, Truman went to bed at his usual time, but Bess and Margaret stayed up all night to listen to the results.

Entertaining during the Truman Administration was very limited. First there was mourning for FDR, then post-World War II food shortages and the Korean War, and finally the complete refurbishment of the White House. The family lived at Blair House during renovation. It was here that Puerto Rican nationalists tried to assassinate Truman. Luckily no member of the Truman family was injured during the attack. Any entertaining was done in nearby hotels or at small intimate dinners at Blair House. Bess had a good memory for names and faces plus a "good tennis elbow" for shaking numerous hands. She often gave teas for servicemen at Blair House, and Margaret and her friends served as waitresses.

Bess and Harry Truman get set to make the trip from Missouri to the White House in this contemporary political cartoon.

Bess was as happy as "the cat that swallowed the canary" when Truman announced he would not be a candidate for reelection in 1952.

Post White House: In retirement, Bess continued with her bridge club, weekly trips to the lending library, and followed baseball games on radio. She and Truman took a six-week tour of Europe in 1952. She participated in the ceremonies opening the Harry S Truman Library and went with Truman to "his office" almost everyday. Bess had a mastectomy in 1959. After one well-publicized babysitting week, she did not watch the grandchildren again but was a doting grandmother.

After Truman died, she lived quietly at home, refusing Margaret's offer to live with her family in New York. She served as honorary chairperson of Thomas Eagleton's 1972 Senate campaign. The other chairperson was baseball great Stan Musial. In her later years she was stricken by arthritis and poor eyesight.

Death: Bess was the longest living of any First Lady, ninety-seven years. She is buried next to Truman at the Harry S Truman Library. Truman wrote her epitaph, Bess Wallace Truman, First Lady of the United States (1945–1953).

MAMIE GENEVA DOUD EISENHOWER

(1896–1979)

First Lady (1953–1961)

The Straight Facts

Born: November 14, 1896
Birthplace: Boone, Iowa
Ancestry: English, Swedish
Physical Characteristics: 5′1″ tall, brown hair, blue eyes
Religion: Presbyterian
Husband: Dwight David Eisenhower (1890–1969)
Date of Marriage: July 1, 1916
Place of Marriage: Denver, Colorado

Children: Two sons
Died: November 1, 1979
Place of Death: Washington, D.C.
Burial Place: Place of Mediation, Dwight D. Eisenhower Center, Abilene, Kansas
White House Portrait: Thomas E. Stephens, East Wing Lobby

The More Colorful Facts

Astrological Sign: Scorpio
Nicknames: Mrs. Ike, Mimi, Sleeping Beauty, Mamie E., First Lady of Femininity
Childhood and Family Life: Mamie was the second of four daughters of meatpacker John Sheldon Doud and Elivera Carlson. Named for Aunt Mary Geneva, she was always called Mamie. She weighed three pounds, six ounces, at birth. Doud ancestors had helped found Guilford, Connecticut. The illness of her sister and mother forced the family to move to Denver, Colorado, when Mamie was nine years old. The family later bought another home in San Antonio, Texas. Mamie attended Jackson, Coronna, and Mulholland Elementary Schools, East Denver High School, and the Wolcott School for Girls. She also attended dancing classes at Miss Hayden's and was once told to curb her enthusiastic dancing style.
Courtship and Marriage: While on a visit to their San Antonio home, the Doud family visited their friends, Major and Mrs Hunter Harris, at Fort Sam Houston. Lulu Harris introduced them to the officer of the watch, recent West Point graduate, 2nd Lt. Dwight D. Eisenhower. Ike was immediately smitten and asked Mamie walk his rounds with him. After they left, Mrs. Harris told the Douds not to worry, as Eisenhower was the "woman hater" of the base. He called that evening and asked for a date. Because she was so popular, Mamie arranged to meet him in three weeks. Ike soon became a familiar face at the Doud home. For her nineteenth birthday he gave her a silver jewelry box. They became engaged on Valentine's Day 1916, and Ike gave her a replica of his West Point ring.

They were married in the parlor of the Doud home in Denver. The nineteen-year-old bride wore a Chantilly lace floor-length dress with tight sleeves and a Bolero jacket. She also wore a pale pink satin cumberbund and carried lilies of the valley and pink baby roses. The twenty-six-year-old groom, newly promoted to 1st Lt., refused to sit for fear of creasing the trousers of his uniform. They honeymooned in Eldorado Springs, Colorado, and Abilene, Kansas, where she met his family.

Children: Mamie had two sons. Dwight D. Eisenhower II, born in 1921, died of scarlet fever at the age of three. He had been nicknamed "Icky" by his father because of the frequent state of his diapers. For the rest of their lives, Ike always sent Mamie flowers on Icky's birthday. John Sheldon Doud Eisenhower (1923-) also went to West Point, served as ambassador to Belgium, and is now a historian.

Personal Notes: Vivacious, out-going Mamie played piano, electric organ, and loved to dance. A weakened heart, the result of rheumatic fever, caused her to prefer indoor activities to outdoor sports. She loved the the game Mah-Jongg and card games such as bolivia, canasta, and whist. She liked mystery novels. Beside her trademark pink, she prefered sunshine yellow in her kitchens. She liked gladioluses. She wore costume jewelry, bright-colored gloves, and flowered dresses. A sentimentalist, she cried at movies, especially love stories and musicals.

Soldier's Wife: The newlyweds' first quarters were two rooms in the officers' barracks at Fort Sam Houston. It was the first of thirty-three homes they lived in during fifty-three years of married life. The first time Ike left Mamie for another assignment, she cried. He told her that he loved her, ". . . but I love my country first." When Ike was stationed at Leon Springs, about twenty miles from San Antonio, she decided to take his old car and visit for the day. Despite the fact that she did not know how to drive, she made the trip successfully until reaching the gate. There, Ike had to jump into the car to get it to stop. She spent the rest of the day learning to drive.

Whenever possible, Mamie traveled with Ike from post to post. She learned a hard lesson when she sold their possessions at one-tenth the value instead of moving them. In 1922, she sailed with him on the SS *Cambria* to Camp Faillard in the Panama Canal Zone. It was here that Mamie cut her hair short and into the famous bangs. In 1936, she and son John sailed on the USS *Ulysses S. Grant* to join Ike in the Philippines when he worked for General Douglas MacArthur. There, in 1938, she had gallbladder surgery. They lived in the Hotel Manila, and their apartment was called the Club Eisenhower because of the gay parties they gave.

During World War II, Mamie lived in Washington at the Wardman Park Hotel and worked in the USO. At one point, she did not see Ike for three years, but they exchanged frequent letters. Her letters were addressed to "My Boyfriend" or "My Favorite Beau" and his were to "the girl (I) love more today than on the day I married you." She kept scrapbooks of Ike's triumphs in Europe and didn't believe the rumors of his affair with British chauffeur Kay Summersby.

After the war, Mamie basked in Ike's glory and rode in the ticker-tape parade with him. He received an honorary degree from Columbia

University in 1947, and Mamie was among those who gave him a standing ovation. Ike stepped out of line and told her, "Don't you ever stand up for me, Mamie." Following a brief stint as president of Columbia University, where they lived at 60 Morningside Drive in New York City, the Eisenhowers traveled to Europe. As supreme commander of NATO, Ike lived with his family at Villa St. Pierre in Marne-la-Coquillière near Paris.

First Lady: It was inevitable that Ike would be a presidential candidate in 1952, but the question was for which party. Ike rarely voted and Mamie had never cast a ballot. Ike decided to run on the Republican ticket, and at the convention, Mamie mingled with delegates, charming them with her infectious smile, which would soon be as famous as Ike's. On a seventy-seven-stop train ride through the country, she appeared with Ike on the platform many times, including once in her bathrobe and curlers. She had little interest in politics but listened to his speech rehearsals and offered advice. He valued her good intuition and shrewd observations.

For the 1953 inauguration, she became a hit with wives when she was seen during a break in the inaugural parade rubbing her sore feet, tired after standing four hours in heels. She wore a Renoir pink, peau de soie inaugural gown by Nettie Rosenstein. Matching shoes and a small clutch purse of the same color completed her outfit.

Mamie proceeded to organize the White House like a good military wife. She planned all aspects of state events, including dress rehearsals, down to the last detail. She usually started her day with breakfast in bed. Then, using the bed as a desk, she planned menus, flower and seating arrangements, and music. She insisted on E-shaped tables so she and Ike could sit next to each other. Mamie was just as meticulous in her housekeeping. She drove the White House staff crazy because she did not like to see footprints on the carpeting.

Most did not know she suffered from a weak heart condition and an inner ear infection called Mèniere's disease. The latter affected her balance and she was often unsteady on her feet, causing rumors of alcoholism. She was claustrophobic and did not enjoy flying. Ike had a piano installed on Air Force One so Mamie could tinker with Chopin etudes to keep her mind off flying.

The Eisenhowers were the first presidential couple of the TV generation. They enjoyed eating dinner on snack trays in front of their set. Their favorite shows were "I Love Lucy," "The Fred Waring Talent Show," and "You Bet Your Life." Mamie's favorite soap opera was "As the World Turns" and she tried to never miss an episode. Mamie took on no social or civic causes as First Lady; her first duty was to Ike. She did selectively lend her name to causes and make appearances.

Leftover flower arrangements from White House dinners were always sent to veterans' hospitals.

When Ike suffered a heart attack in 1955, Mamie moved into the hospital to be with him. She personally answered every letter of good wishes for the president in turquoise ink. Mamie was against his running for a second term. She spent most of the second term commuting to Gettysburg, Pennsylvania, where they were building their retirement home. It was to be the only home they ever owned together. She supervised renovation and made almost all decoration decisions.

Post White House: In retirement, the Eisenhowers celebrated their fiftieth wedding anniversary. She continued her custom of having a masseuse three times a week, going to Elizabeth Arden's, and having card parties. During Ike's final illness, she moved into Walter Reed Army Hospital to be with him during the final months of his life. After Ike's death, she continued to work on his causes and promote his name. She went to his grave site every year and attended the yearly graduation ceremonies at Eisenhower College. In 1974, she attended the dedication of Eisenhower Hall at West Point. In 1977, she helped christen the supercarrier USS *Dwight D. Eisenhower*. After Ike's death, she and her Secret Service agents always wore an American flag in their lapels in tribute. Before her death, Mamie granted an interview to Barbara Walters, which was aired the week after she died.

Death: Mamie died of cardiac arrest two weeks shy of her eighty-third birthday. She had been rushed to Walter Reed Army Hospital a few weeks earlier. She is buried next to her husband and their infant son in the Place of Mediation at the Dwight D. Eisenhower Center in Abilene, Kansas.

Honors/Honorary Degrees

Colorado Womens College, 1946
Cavalier Order of the Southern Cross (Brazil), 1946
Dress Institute, Best Dressed Roster, 1952
Order of Malta (Italy), 1952
Grand Cross, Order of Honor and Men (Cuba), 1953
St. Joseph College, 1959
Heart of the Year Award, 1960
Iowa Award, 1970

JACQUELINE LEE BOUVIER KENNEDY

(1929–)

First Lady (1961–1963)

The Straight Facts

Born: July 28, 1929
Birthplace: Southampton, New York
Ancestry: French, Irish
Physical Characteristics: 5'7" tall, auburn hair, brown eyes
Religion: Roman Catholic
Husbands: (1) John Fitzgerald Kennedy (1917–1963)
(2) Aristotle Socrates Onassis (1906–1975)

Date of Marriages: (1) September 12, 1953
(2) October 22, 1968
Place of Marriages: (1) Newport, Rhode Island
(2) Skorpios Island, Greece
Children: (1) Two sons, one daughter
(2) None
Firsts: To be born in twentieth century
To give birth to the child of a president-elect
To serve as First Lady in her thirties
To give a televised tour of the White House
To be received by the Pope
White House Portrait: Aaron Shikler, ground floor corridor

The More Colorful Facts

Astrological Sign: Leo
Nicknames: Jackie, Queen of America, Jacqueline Borgia, Ameriki Rani
Childhood and Family Life: Jacqueline (pronounced Jack-leen) Lee Bouvier
is the privileged eldest daughter of financier John Vernou Bouvier III
(Black Jack) and Janet Lee. Devoted to her father, she was devastated
by her parents' 1940 divorce. Self-assured at a young age, four-year-old
Jacqueline was separated from her nurse one day in the park. She went
up to a police officer who asked her if she was lost. She said no, but her
nurse was.

She attended school at Holton-Arms (1942–1944), Miss Porter's
(1944–1947), Vassar College (1947–1948), the Sorbonne (1949), and
earned her art degree from George Washington University in 1951.
She won the *Vogue* magazine Prix de Paris award, which included a
year's study in France, but turned it down. The contest involved writing an essay on the three people you would most like to meet. Jacqueline selected Charles Baudelaire, Oscar Wilde, and Sergei Diaghilev.

She made her society debut in 1947 at the Clambake Club. Columnist Cholly Knickerbocker (Igor Cassini) selected Jacqueline as the
"Queen Deb of the Year."
Career Girl: Family friend Arthur Krock arranged for Jacqueline to be employed by the *Washington Times Herald* as its Inquiring Camera Girl
for $42.50 per week, plus camera and film. Her job was to ask ques-
tions of people on the street and to interview prominent Washingto-
nians and take pictures of those who responded. Her first interview
subject was the wife of then vice-president, Pat Nixon.
Courtship and Marriage: John Kennedy met his future wife at a dinner held
in the home of columnist Charles Bartlett. Kennedy always said he

"reached across the asparagus and asked her for a date." Jacqueline always retorted that there was no asparagus served that night. He did escort her back to her car after dinner and both were surprised to find one of her boyfriends sitting in the back seat. He had seen the car and decided to surprise her. JFK made a hasty retreat and Jacqueline was furious with her "surprise." Their dating was sporadic as JFK was often away campaigning. She was JFK's date at the 1952 Eisenhower inauguration. They became engaged to become engaged but she could not get JFK to set a date. She even took her campaign public by asking interview questions like "Do you think a bachelor is truly happy?"; "Is your marriage a fifty-fifty partnership, or do you feel you give more?"; and more pointedly, "The Irish author Sean O'Faolain claims that the Irish are deficient in the art of love. Do you agree with the author's opinion?"

Jacqueline covered the coronation of Queen Elizabeth II for the newspaper and Jack sent her a wire saying that he missed her. He also sent her on a shopping expedition for certain books he wanted. She searched all over London to find the books. They were too heavy to meet customs standards, and she sent him the bill for the extra duty. He finally proposed, but they delayed announcing their engagement as JFK was soon to appear on the cover of the *Saturday Evening Post,* in an article entitled "Jack Kennedy, the Senate's Gay Young Bachelor."

Their marriage was the social event of the year. Over 800 guests (including the entire Senate) were invited to the Catholic high mass ceremony. The Archbishop Richard Cushing officiated. (Caroline) Lee Bouvier Canfield served as her sister's matron of honor and Robert F. Kennedy served as best man; there were twelve other attendants on each side. The bride was given away by stepfather Hugh D. Auchincloss as Black Jack had overslept after a night of heavy prewedding drinking. The reception was held at Hammersmith Farms, the Auchincloss es seventy-five-acre summer estate and 1,200 guests were invited. The twenty-four-year-old bride wore an ivory white taffeta gown with a full bouffant skirt. She wore her maternal grandmother's rose point veil held in place with a coronet of orange blossoms, with only a single strand of white pearls. The couple honeymooned in Acapulco.

Children: The Kennedy's two young children provided much interest and entertainment during the couple's White House years. Caroline Bouvier (1957–), now Mrs. Edwin Arthur Schlossberg and the mother of Rose Kennedy Schlossberg (1988–), rode her pony, Macaroni, on the White House lawn and attended kindergarten classes in a third-floor room. John F. Kennedy Jr. (1960–) is the first child born to a president-elect. Nicknamed "John-John" by the press, he was only three when his father died. Both Caroline and John are lawyers. The Kennedys also had a stillborn daughter in 1956 and lost son Patrick Bouvier after three days of life in 1963.

Personal Notes: Jacqueline does not like to be called Jackie. She is a natural horsewoman who has been riding since the age of two. As a child she won numerous riding medals and ribbons. She walks, jogs, and enjoys water sports. She is an ardent supporter of the arts with French Impressionist paintings, the ballet, and classical string music her favorites. She paints in oils and watercolors and loves animals.

She likes lime daiquiris and personally distributed her preferred recipe to the White House staff. A favorite lunch is a baked potato filled with caviar. She is an avid reader and enjoys poetry with favorites being Robert Frost and Alfred de Musset. She speaks French, Italian, Spanish, and some Greek. She is naturally shy and guards her privacy. Even as First Lady she gave few interviews. Outside of a large gathering each summer and family occasions such as weddings, births, etc., she has shied away from Kennedy family affairs. At the famous family touch football games, Jacqueline stayed on the sidelines, talking with father-in-law Joseph P. Kennedy. She refused to participate in the games after she was reportedly run over and ended up with a broken ankle the first time she played.

Politician's Wife: Before (and after) she married she had little interest in politics. She did not get involved with political affairs and did not work at her husband's office as other wives had done. She claimed her number-one responsibility was her husband and, when the time came, children. She attended few meetings of the Senate Wives Club. In 1956 and 1958, she made few appearances for JFK's Senate races.

During 1960, she campaigned openly for the first time, despite being pregnant. She appeared on "The Dave Garroway Show" and made personal appearances across the country. In Milwaukee, in her whispery little-girl voice, Jacqueline appealed to shoppers in a grocery store, over the store loudspeaker, to vote for JFK. In the *barrios,* she spoke in Spanish; in the bayous, she spoke French; in New York, she impressed voters with her fashion sense. After seeing the poverty in West Virginia, she vowed to help as First Lady, which she did by buying glasses made at the Morgantown Glass Works.

She once accompanied JFK when he made an appearance on "Face the Nation." Jacqueline personally handed each panelist a note which read "Please Don't Ask Jack Mean Questions." And in November 1960, for the first time in her life, she voted. "I voted just for Jack and no one else."

First Lady: At thirty-one years of age, Jacqueline became the thirty-first First Lady. Her glamour, grace, and charm were a welcoming change in Washington. The beautiful people were back in and the Ken-

nedys asked guests from all walks of life to the White House. With the help of social secretary Letitia Baldridge, Jacqueline graced the executive mansion with artists, musicians, and political leaders. She also persuaded the board of governors overseeing Mt. Vernon to allow a reception for a visiting head of state at the first president's home.

As before, she claimed her main responsibilties were to her husband and children. But, after moving into the mansion, she chose as her special project restoration of the White House. With a committee of ten, she selected works of art and furniture for the White House. Her main tenet was that everything must have a reason for being there. The new furniture also included two chairs made by ancestor Michel Bouvier in 1820. Funds for the renovation came from private donations and the sale of a guide book about the White House. The crowning glory of the renovation was the February 1962 televised broadcast of "A Tour of the White House with Mrs. John F. Kennedy." It is estimated that over fifty-six million people watched the show, which featured a "surprise" visit from the president. CBS planned on scheduling three days to tape the show. It took seven hours.

Jacqueline's fashion sense made her a sensation everywhere ever she went. She favored stack-heeled pumps, sleeveless dresses, and, at times, capri pants for daytime wear. She liked pillbox hats, stiff-han-

dled purses, and collarless coats. Her tastes were varied when it came
to evening wear but, whatever design was chosen it was elegant and in
good taste.

She traveled with JFK to Europe in 1961. The French extensively
cheered "Jacqui" and JFK remarked, "I am the man who accompanied Jacqueline Kennedy to Europe and I have enjoyed it." She
charmed Charles deGaulle by telling him, in French, that she had read
his autobiography. She also took trips on her own. In 1962, she and sister Lee took a trip to India and Asia. On the way, they stopped in Rome
to have a private audience with Pope John XXIII. In India she was a
treated like a queen, rode an elephant, and was appalled at the poverty.
Following Patrick's death in 1963, she and Lee took a month-long
cruise in the Mediterranean as the guests of Greek shipping magnate
Aristotle Onassis.

She made the final campaign trip with JFK to Dallas in 1963.
Many of his staff were surprised she went and that she was enjoying
herself. The night before his death, Jacqueline promised she would
campaign for him in the 1964 election.

During the four days of the Kennedy assassination drama, Jacqueline was a symbol of the world's sorrow and pain. No one will forget
her blood-splattered pink suit, her crawling on the trunk of the limousine, her standing next to Lyndon Johnson while he took the oath, or
the funeral. She made most of the arrangements herself, insisting it be
as much like Abraham Lincoln's as possible. She selected the Arlington
site and it was her decision to have the eternal flame. Upon the return
from Arlington, she went upstairs with her children to celebrate their
birthdays.

Post White House: Upon leaving the White House in December, Jacqueline
and her children moved to Georgetown, just a few doors down from
where they had lived before entering the presidential mansion. She
oversaw the acknowledgment of the many cards of condolence and
gathered papers to be placed in the Kennedy Library. Her first public
appearance was a televised expression of thanks to the people of the
country for their outpouring of support and love. She also made a brief
appearance at the 1964 Democratic Convention but did no campaigning for Lyndon Johnson.

For the next few years, she tried to live quietly and raise her children with little fuss. She traveled to dedication ceremonies for monu-
ments that honored JFK, including a trip to England where a memorial
stone was laid at historic Runnymede. The family moved to New York,
where they hoped to obtain more privacy, but, no matter where they
went, the paparazzi found them. Jacqueline even went so far as to get a

court order barring photographer Ron Gallela from shooting her picture from within 1,000 feet of her.

Jacqueline celebrated her sixtieth birthday in 1989 with much-publicized recollections of her life. Each year numerous books and articles appear about the Kennedys indicating that the aura surrounding them has not died. She is currently employed by Doubleday as a book editor. Coworkers give her high marks for always being prepared, thorough in her research, and knowledgeable in the subject matter she is dealing with. Her most noted book was one written by rock star Michael Jackson; she personally persuaded him to publish it.

Her social life still involves extensive travel. After JFK's death, she was escorted by members of the "Irish Mafia" or other close friends, including Lord Harlech of Britain. For the last ten years, her escort has been New Yorker Maurice Tempelsman.

Second Husband: Five years after JFK's death she married Greek shipping tycoon Aristotle Onassis in Skorpios, Greece. The ceremony was held at the Church of the Holy Virgin. The groom was twenty-three years older than the thirty-nine-year-old bride, who wore a beige dress and single ribbon in her hair. The two Kennedy and two Onassis children were in attendance. The world was outraged at the union, thinking she married Onassis only for his money and had harmed JFK's memory. For marrying a divorced man, she was excommunicated from the Catholic church. Former mother-in-law Rose Kennedy sent her congratulations on the match, knowing how lonely Jacqueline had been.

Onassis settled a large amount of money on her in the prenuptial agreement and set up trust funds for both of her children. She was given a generous clothing allowance and access to his entire holdings. Theirs was a commuter marriage as she lived in New York most of the time. At the time of Onassis' death they were semi-separated.

CLAUDIA ALTA TAYLOR JOHNSON

(1912–)

First Lady 1963–1969

The Straight Facts

Born: December 12, 1912
Birthplace: Karnack, Texas
Ancestry: Scots, Spanish, English
Physical Characteristics: 5'6" tall, black hair, brown eyes
Religion: Episcopalian
Husband: Lyndon Baines Johnson (1908–1973)
Date of Marriage: November 17, 1934
Place of Marriage: San Antonio, Texas
Children: Two daughters
Firsts: To be born in Texas
To hold the Bible for husband's inauguration
To go on the campaign trail for her husband on her own

To give a state dinner in the White House Rose Garden
To own a radio station
White House Portrait: Elizabeth Shoumatoff, ground floor corridor

The More Colorful Facts

Astrological Sign: Sagittarius
Nickname: Lady Bird, Gentle Hand, Nini
Childhood and Family Life: Lady Bird is the daughter of merchant/politician Thomas Jefferson Taylor and his cultured wife, Minnie Lee Pattillo. Christened Claudia Alta, she was delivered by Dr. Benjamin Baldwin. Family nursemaid Alice Tittle was responsible for the nickname as she thought the baby was "as purty as a little lady bird." Her mother died before she was five and her maternal aunt, Effie Pattillo, came from Alabama to help raise her. She finished third in her class at Marshal High School, was graduated from St. Mary's Junior College for Girls, and received a BA in 1933 from the University of Texas in journalism. While there, she qualified for a teacher's certificate.
Courtship and Marriage: While dining at the home of family friend Eugene Lassiter, she met the aide to Congressman Dick Kleburg, Lyndon Baines Johnson. He was immediately smitten, and as he already had a date for the evening, asked Miss Taylor to meet him for breakfast the next morning. She did not reply to his request, but "just happened" to show up at the Hotel Driskill the next morning at the appointed time. He proposed that afternoon and two months later they were married. She had always wanted to have her wedding at St. Mark's Episcopal Church in San Antonio and she got her wish. The pastor, the Rev. Arthur K. McKinstry officiated. Cecille Harrison and Henry A. Hirshberg served as witnesses. The nervous twenty-six-year-old bridegroom remembered the license (Bexar County License #104133), but forgot the ring. He sent Hirshberg down to Sears for a plain gold band, which cost $2.98. After the ceremony, LBJ forgot to pick up the signed license, and it wasn't until thirty-four years later when President and Mrs. Johnson visited San Antonio, that it was returned to them. They honeymooned in Mexico.
Children: After several miscarriages, Lady Bird had two daughters. Lynda Bird (1944–) married Marine Major (now Senator) Charles S. Robb in a 1967 White House ceremony. Luci (1947–) married Patrick Nugent in 1966 and has four children; they divorced in 1979. She married Ian Turpin in 1984.
Personal Notes: Vivacious Lady Bird is a historian who is fluent in Spanish. A longtime conservationist, her favorite flowers are peonies and blue

bonnets. Her favorite color is yellow. She is also fond of peanut brittle and would hide a box under her bed away from LBJ's eyes. She loves the classics and claims her first love was the legendary hero, Siegfried. She also loved the television show "Gunsmoke" and had it taped if she could not watch it in person. She said its star, Jim Arness, reminded her of LBJ. When informed that Arness was a Republican, she still watched the show but didn't make the reference to LBJ anymore.

Politician's Wife: The newlyweds lived in a one-bedroom Washington apartment at 1910 Kalorama Road. She helped Lyndon entertain Congressman Kleberg's constituents and gave sightseeing tours. When LBJ decided to enter the 1937 congressional race, she supported him and loaned him $10,000 from her inheritance to get started. She stayed in the background, working only in the headquarters because that was the role of a political wife in those days. After LBJ won, she helped him in the office and memorized the names of all the counties in his district, their seats, and key politicians in the area. She served as his sounding board on ideas and helped with the correspondence. In 1941, they attended a reception in the White House for the Duchess of Luxembourg. Lady Bird wrote in her diary that it would probably be her only visit to the White House.

During World War II, she served as liason between the uniformed LBJ and his constituents. She also bought radio station KTBC, and within a year, turned it into a profitable venture. After the war, LBJ decided to run for the Senate. This time, Lady Bird was an active participant. She made speeches, handled mail, recruited her entire family to make phone calls, and supervised the campaign workers. One night on a way to deliver a speech, the car in which she was riding skidded in the mud and overturned twice. She and her companion hitched a ride, she borrowed a dress, made her speech, and then went to the hospital for X- rays. Her only thought as the car overturned was "I wish I had voted absentee."

The new senator and his family lived at 4040 52nd Street NW, called the Elms. They also bought what is now the LBJ Ranch on the Pedernales River in Texas. In 1952, Lady Bird bought KTBC-TV in Austin, Texas. The Johnsons were popular in Washington social circles. Lady Bird was a gracious and charming hostess who could discuss politics. When LBJ was elected majority leader, their home became busier than ever. Her witty, friendly, feminine style scored many points for his career.

When LBJ suffered a heart attack in 1955, she took the room next to his in the hospital to aid his convalescence. When LBJ declared for president in 1960, she held her first press conference. As the wife of the vice-presidential candidate, she was an integral part of the campaign

team. She traveled over 35,000 miles and was called the "Secret Weapon." Robert Kennedy always claimed that it was Lady Bird and not Lyndon that carried Texas for them in the race.

As the wife of the vice-president, she set three goals: (1) To help LBJ; (2) to help Jacqueline Kennedy; and (3) to be more alive. She pinch-hit for the First Lady at White House functions and even accepted Jackie's Emmy, given for the televised White House tour. Lady Bird traveled over 120,000 miles and to thirty countries. In November 1963, the Johnsons invited the Kennedys to a barbecue at the LBJ Ranch after a four-day tour of Texas. They joined the presidential party in a tour of San Antonio, Fort Worth, and Dallas.

First Lady: It was a somber Lady Bird who took up residence in the White House after the Kennedy family moved out. She said she felt as if she should "tiptoe" around, not really believing she was there. When they started to entertain, the events were friendly, open affairs often taking the form of a carnival, barbecue, or hootenanny. She was the first First Lady to actively use the White House bowling alley. Her locker was #17 and she bowled a 128 average.

During the campaign of 1964, she undertook her own whistlestop tour of the south. "The Lady Bird Special" departed on a 1,682-mile, forty-seven-stop, and four-slowdown tour. Dressed in a bright red coat, Lady Bird rode in car #2 and enticed other politicians to join the tour.

Comfortable as First Lady in her own right, she set out to campaign for her pet cause—conservation. The First Lady's Committee For a More Beautiful Capital and the White House Conference on Natural Beauty were formed. The Highway Beautification Act of 1965 was dubbed the "Lady Bird Act." She advocated the Discover America program and traveled around the country to promote the beautification of the landscape. On one of these so called "Lady Bird Safaris" she took a four-day trip in a raft down the Saddle River. The press dubbed her the "Lone Ranger" on these trips.

Lady Bird was assisted by social secretary Bess Abell and press secretary Liz Carpenter. LBJ often impulsively invited guests without telling her. Both Johnson daughters held wedding receptions at the White House. Lady Bird's office door at the White House bore a large sign that read "MRS. JOHNSON AT WORK." No one can recall hearing an unkind remark about her and the Secret Service dubbed her "Victoria." She made numerous visits to hospitals, nursing homes, and schools. She would place her arms around the most despondent and whisper in their ear, "Remember dear, you are loved."

On a trip to Cleveland, Ohio, for the dedication of the Riverview Senior Center, her plane developed difficulties; it was decided to drive back to Washington. Liz Carpenter called ahead and they stopped for dinner at Howard Johnson's outside Pittsburgh. After the First Lady and her party left, reporters asked the waitress how she felt about serving the First Lady. The woman was shocked when she found out it was Lady Bird. She said she was nervous enough when she thought she was serving Mrs. Howard Johnson.

Post White House: Since leaving the White House, Lady Bird has continued her beautification and conservation efforts. She appeared in the 1976 Salute to America effort and campaigned for son-in-law Chuck Robb in his campaigns for governor and then senator. She has also worked on the development of the Lyndon Baines Johnson Library and Museum in Austin, Texas. In 1988, she moved to Austin to be near the library but also maintains the LBJ Ranch which she calls her Serengeti. She has already written her own epitaph "She Planted Three Trees."

Boards

The National Wildflower Research Center
National Geographic Society
National Park Service
American Conservation Association
University of Texas Regents

Honors/Honorary Degrees

University of Texas, 1964
Texas Women's College, 1964
Middleburg College, 1967
Williams College, 1967
Southwestern University, 1967
Presidential Medal of Freedom, 1977
Congressional Gold Medal of Freedom, 1988

THELMA CATHERINE (PATRICIA) RYAN NIXON
(1912–)
First Lady (1969–1974)

The Straight Facts

Born: March 16, 1912
Birthplace: Ely, Nevada
Ancestry: Irish, German
Physical Characteristics: 5'6" tall, red hair, blue eyes
Religion: Congregationalist
Husband: Richard Milhous Nixon (1913–)
Date of Marriage: June 21, 1940
Place of Marriage: Riverside, California
Children: Two daughters

Firsts: To be born in Nevada
To appear in movies
To illuminate the White House at night
To visit China
To represent the U.S. at the inauguration of a foreign leader
White House Portrait: Henriette Wyeth Hurd, ground floor corridor

The More Colorful Facts

Astrological Sign: Pisces
Nicknames: Pat, Fair Lady, Babe, Buddy, PluPlastic Pat, Antiseptic Pat, Pat the Robot
Childhood and Family Life: Thelma Catharine Ryan was the youngest child of widow Katharina (Kate) Halberstadt Bender and her second husband, miner/farmer William Ryan. She had two older brothers and an older half-brother and half-sister from her mother's first marriage. Returning home from working a midnight shift, Will was surprised with his "St. Patty's Babe in the Morning." When Will decided to try his hand at farming, the family moved to Artesia (now Cerritos), California. The whole family chipped in to try to make the ten-acre truck farm work. Pat's mother died when she was fourteen; in addition to her other chores, she was now housekeeper. Her father died when she was a senior at Excelsior High School. She decided to change her name to Patricia in his honor. Despite the hard work at home, she graduated near the top of her class, served as vice-president of both the student body and of Les Marionettes, the school drama society.
Teacher: After high school, she attended Fullerton Junior College and supported herself by working as a cleaning lady and bank clerk. She quit the latter job after being handed a robbery note. When the opportunity to chauffer an elderly couple to New York in exchange for a return bus ticket emerged, she jumped at the chance. In New York, she worked for two years at Seton Hospital as an X-ray technician. Returning to Los Angeles, she worked her way through the University of Southern California with numerous jobs including acting bits in Hollywood movies. She graduated *cum laude* in 1934 with a degree in merchandising and a teacher's certificate. She took a job at nearby Whittier High School teaching shorthand, typing, and government. Among her students was future CBS newsman Robert Pierpoint. She also coached the pep squad and the cheerleaders. In her spare time, she participated in the local community theatre.
Courtship and Marriage: Pat won the part of Daphne in the Alexander Wollcott-George S. Kaufman play *The Dark Tower*. She played opposite a

young lawyer named Richard Nixon. Nixon was instantly attracted to the young teacher and asked her out. She declined, saying she was much too busy. He then told her he was going to marry her someday, to which she laughed.

They finally started dating. When she went out with someone else, Nixon often drove her to her date, waited around, and then drove her home again.They went picnicking, dancing, skating, and riding around town. He helped her grade papers, wrote poetry to her, and sent her flowers. Nixon slipped an engagement ring in a May Day basket in 1940 and presented it to her at Dana Point park.

They were married at the Mission Inn in Riverside, California, by the president of Whittier College, who was also a Quaker elder. The twenty-eight-year-old bride wore a light blue dress with a fitted bodice and a full skirt, and a small pink hat. Her only flower was a white orchid, The couple honeymooned in Mexico. To save money, they brought along canned goods but mischievous friends had removed all the labels. They had beans for breakfast and pineapple for dinner. They returned to a small apartment at 12326 E. Beverly Blvd., in Whittier.

Children: The Nixons have two daughters. Patricia, called Tricia (1946–), married Edward Cox in the only outdoor wedding at the White House; they have one son. Julie (1948–) married Dwight David Eisenhower II in 1968; they have three children. Both the Eisenhowers are authors and among their works are books on their famous families.

Personal Notes: Pat is a very private person devoted to her family. She is much better with one-on-one contacts; she believes you can build stronger relationships that way than with a crowd. She believes breakfast is the most relaxing part of the day. Although activities have been somewhat limited by her current physical condition, she likes to sew, garden, and take long walks. She loves dogs but puts her foot down when Nixon lets them lie on the furniture. An avid reader, her favorites are historicals novels, biographies, and anything by Taylor Caldwell. She loves the theatre, operettas, and New York's Frick Museum.

Naval Wife: During World War II, Pat worked for the Office of Price Administration as a price analyst in the San Francisco office. While Nixon was in the South Pacific, they wrote to each other every day.

Politician's Wife: Still in uniform, Nixon was chosen to run for the 12th Congressional District Seat in his hometown as a Republican. Pat was a Democrat who quickly switched parties. She was not much interested in politicis but agreed it was worth the chance. They invested their entire life savings of $10,000 in the race. Pat practically ran the campaign office singlehandedly, stuffing envelopes, making phone calls, and recruting volunteers, despite the fact that she was pregnant. In exchange for helping Nixon with the campaign, she solicited a promise that she would never have to make a campaign speech and could stay home and make as normal a home as possible for her children.

To the surpise of many, Nixon won. Tha family moved to Washington, where they rented a small apartment at 338 Gunston Road. Pat tried to stay out of the limelight. She attended Congressional Wives Club meetings and helped at Nixon's office. Mostly she stayed home with the children. To ensure that they had time with their father, Pat would arrange "picnics" on the floor of his office complete with blankets and beach towels.

During the 1952 Republican National Convention in Chicago, she was lunching in a restaurant when the news broke over the radio that Dwight Eisenhower had selected Nixon as his vice-presidential running mate. Pat says she practically spit out her sandwhich and rushed to the convention hall. She did no campaigning on her own and she made no speeches, but she did make many appearances with her husband. The news of a secret "slush fund" appeared to doom Nixon's candidacy. Pat urged him to fight back and confront the issue head on. She sat quietly next to him as he made his famous "Checkers" speech. In it, he mentioned her three times, including the reference to the now famous "respectable Republican cloth coat." The speech was a success; this was borne out by the avalanche of supporting telegrams. But she was disturbed that Ike took so long to confirm his support.

In the first vice-presidential term, the Nixons lived at 4811 Tilden Street NW, in Washington's Spring Valley section. During the second term, they lived at 4308 Forest Lane in the more fashionable Wesley Heights suburb. The second-youngest vice-president and his family were good subjects for the news media. Inquiring Camera Girl Jackie Bouvier asked little Tricia if she ever played with Democrats. Tricia wanted to know what a Democrat was. The media could not believe that the wife of a vice-president cooked, sewed, and ironed her husband's pants.

Pat was the most traveled of all vice-presidential wives, visiting over fifty-three countries. The State Department gave her high marks for doing research before each trip. She wanted to know about the people and customs as well as the political and economic conditions in each country. She insisted time be set aside in the offical schedule to include visits to schools, hospitals, and orphanages. Her greatest test came during a 1958 visit to Venezuela, where an angry crowd attacked the vice-presidential motorcade. Pat remembers feeling anger at the demonstrators for treating guests to their country in such a manner. Only later did she remember to be scared.

During the 1960 presidential campaign, she was again a visible but nonvocal participant in the campaign. The whistlestop campaign train that had worked so well for Truman and Eisenhower was called the "Dick and Pat Nixon Special." The Republican Party held a Pat Nixon for First Lady Week resulting in an unprecedent thirteen official political buttons for a presidential candidate's wife.

After the narrow defeat, which saw a tearful Pat appear on camera when Nixon conceded, the family returned to California. They settled in an exclusive suburb of Los Angeles and began to lead what Pat called normal lives. She was against Nixon entering the 1962 California gubenatorial race and felt there was no way he could win the election. She was right.

In 1963, they moved to New York and a Fifth Avenue apartment. Nixon joined a law firm, and Pat and the girls enjoyed the museums and theatre. They also traveled extensively as Nixon began to prepare for a 1968 presidential run. Once, when Pat and her friend, Louise Johnson, registered at a hotel, they caused a sensation because the management thought they had Mrs. Nixon and Mrs. Lyndon Johnson in residence. For the rest of the trip, Pat called her friend Louise Bird.

First Lady: The first day in the White House, the new First Lady caused a minor problem in the kitchen. The chefs had stocked what was believed to be the Nixons' favorite foods. For her first meal, she ordered a bowl of cottage cheese. They had to go to three stores before they found one with cottage cheese. Thereafter, the kitchen was never without it.

Pat did much to give the American people better access to the White House. Tours were given to the blind, the hearing impaired, and the physically disabled. She invited people from all walks of life to receptions, wanting more than just celebrities and those with power. The Nixons hosted an outdoor reception for returned Vietnam POWs and their wives. She catalogued the White House artwork and china services. She also had the White House illuminated at night so that more people could see its beauty. The first time Nixon flew by the White House in the evening, he had the pilot circle the mansion four times. For this, the Secret Service dubbed her "Starlight."

Pat spent four hours a day answering mail. Instead of one particular cause, she advocated volunteerism. That way, more organizations would receive the benefit of the experiences of others. She spent many hours visiting nursing homes, hospitals, schools, and orphanages.

She traveled to eighty-three countries as good-will ambassador, and even made a few trips on her own. She flew relief supplies to Peru to help accident victims. The plane was a military transport and she sat on a kitchen chair. She visited famine victims in Africa.

During the 1972 presidential campaign, she even gave a few campaign speeches. She toured seven states on her own and was well received. During the second term, she invited Jacqueline Kennedy and her children to the White House for a private unveiling of the official Kennedy presidential portrait. Jacqueline agreed as long as there was no press allowed to witness the ceremony. Pat agreed and after the ceremony took the family on a tour to show them the changes that had been made. Helen Thomas of UPI found out about the visit and agreed not to print the story until the Kennedys left.

Activities during the last term were clouded by Watergate. Pat was a staunch supporter of her husband and had little to say publicly about the scandal. In private, she said that had if it been her, she would have burned the tapes. She knew the end was near when Nixon advised her to cancel the order for new china.

Post White House: Leaving the White House, the Nixons returned to their San Clemente, California, home located at 4100 Calla Isabell Drive, nicknamed La Casa Pacifica. Worried about Nixon's mental and physical health, Pat took great pains to set his room up first. In 1974, Pat suffered the first of three strokes, which partially paralyzed her left side. She has since made a slow, painful recovery. She was well enough to attend the dedication of the Patricia Ryan Nixon Elementary School in Cerritos in 1975.

The Nixons later moved to Saddle River, New Jersey, to be near their grandchildren. Pat divides her time between walking, swimming, gardening, and reading. And, true to form, she grants no interviews. The American people reveal a deep affection for Pat despite what their feelings may be for her husband. She is the only woman to appear in the top ten of *Good Housekeeping* magazine's Most Admired Woman list since its inception.

Daughter Julie wrote a biography of her mother entitled *Pat Nixon: The Untold Story*. In an amusing aftermath, Pat was at Elizabeth Arden's in New York having her hair done. A woman rushed up to her and said, "Oh, Mrs. Eisenhower, I just loved the book about your mother."

Honors/Honorary Degrees:
University of California, 1961
Grand Cross, Order of the Sun (Peru), 1971
Grand Cordon, Most Venerable Order of Knighthood Pioneers (Liberia), 1972
Gift of Life, Hadassah, 1973
Molly Pitcher Award, Women's Forum
Queen Olha Medal, Womens Association for the Defense of the Four Freedoms

ElIZABETH ANN BLOOMER WARREN FORD

(1918–)

First Lady (1974–1977)

The Straight Facts

Born: April 18, 1918
Birthplace: Chicago, Illinois
Ancestry: English
Physical Characteristics: Brown hair, brown eyes
Religion: Episcopalian
Husbands: (1) William Warren
          (2) Gerald Rudolph Ford (1913–)
Date of Marriages: (2) October 15, 1948
Place of Marriages: (2) Grand Rapids, Michigan
Children: (2) Three sons, one daughter
Firsts: To be born in Illinois
        To have an operation for cancer as First Lady
White House Portrait: Felix de Cossio, ground floor corridor

The More Colorful Facts

Astrological Sign: Aries

Nicknames: Betty, Betts, Skipper, Petunia

Childhood and Family Life: Betty was the youngest child of industrial supply salesman William Stephenson Bloomer and Hortense Nehr. Her mother always told Betty that she popped out like a champagne cork. A chubby tomboy, she would often tramp along in the woods with her brothers and their pet shepherd Teddy. Mrs. Bloomer was concerned about her daughter's weight and hung a sign that read "Please Do Not Feed This Child" when Betty went out to play. She attended Central High School, where she was a popular member of the Gamma Delta Tau sorority. The group was also known as the "Good Cheers." Before she graduated from high school, her alcoholic father died of carbon monoxide poisoning in the family garage.

Dancer: As a child she took dance lessons at the Calla Travis Dance Studio, and before too long, she was also teaching. After high school graduation, Betty went to the Bennington School of Dance in Vermont. She also joined the auxiliary troupe of the Martha Graham Dance Studio. In New York, she also modeled for the John Robert Powers Agency. After two years, she returned to Grand Rapids where she opened her own dance studio.

First Marriage: Betty married insurance man William C. Warren in 1942. She continued to teach dance but was also working full time as an assistant fashion coordinator for Herpolsheimer's Department Store. Warren quit his job and tried his hand at selling furniture but couldn't make a go of it. Marital problems arose and Betty threatened to leave him because of his alcoholism. When it was discovered he had diabetes, she stayed with Warren for another year before finally leaving him.

Courtship and Marriage: Before the divorce was final, Betty started dating again. A friend called and asked her if she would go out with former Grand Rapids high school football great Gerald Ford who was back in town. Betty said she didn't have time. When pressed, she agreed to meet him for twenty minutes; the visit stretched over an hour. After a nine-month courtship, he proposed in February 1948. After she accepted, he told her they could not announce their engagement or get married until the fall and he couldn't tell her why. In June, she found out why. He simultaneously announced his engagement to Betty and his candidacy for the open congressional seat in his district.

They were married three weeks before the election at the Grace Episcopal Church. The previous evening, the Fords hosted a rehearsal dinner at the Peninsula Club. The twenty-year-old bride wore a sapphire blue satin dress with matching hat and shoes. She carried American Beauty roses. The thirty-five-year-old groom was late due to campaigning and had mud on his shoes. Thus was born the rumor that he wore one black and one brown shoe. They honeymooned in Ann Arbor at the Allenel Hotel. Betty would stay no higher than the second floor because she thought the hotel looked like a firetrap.

Children: Betty had no children by her first marriage and four by her second. Michael (1950–) is a minister. John, known as Jack (1952–), works in the communications industry. Steven (1956–) is an actor. Susan (1957–) is the divorced mother of two

Politician's Wife: The newlywed congressman Ford and wife rented a small apartment at 2500 Q Street in Georgetown. Each set out on a learning experience of how Washington works, Ford from the congressional side, Betty from the spousal side. But there were no rule books or even suggestion books for wives. She worked at Ford's office handling mail, escorting constituents and entertaining at receptions. Bess Truman invited the wives of new congressmen to tea at Blair House. On the chosen day, a terrible rainstorm erupted. A very pregnant and very nervous Betty greeted the First Lady and thanked her for the invitation. Bess set Betty at ease by thanking her for attending in such terrible weather. It was the beginning of a mutual admiration that lasted over twenty-five years even though they were on opposite political sides.

As the children arrived and Ford rose up congressional ranks, Betty stayed home and ran the household. She served as den mother, Sunday school teacher, and PTA volunteer. One year, they estimated that Ford spent 258 nights away from their home. They soon moved to 5014 Crown View Drive in Alexandria. Betty was very involved with the Alexandria Cancer Fund.

In 1973, she lost a $5.00 bet to daughter Susan when Ford was selected by President Nixon to succeed Spiro Agnew as vice-president. During the eight months Ford served as vice-president, Betty did some entertaining, but little traveling. She was not prepared for Nixon's resignation.

First Lady: Betty had a full schedule her first week as First Lady because the Fords had inherited the Nixons' social schedule. There were two state dinners, and twelve official appearances. There was also a household to close up and one to set up. In contrast to shy Pat Nixon, Americans found themselves with a different, outspoken First Lady who was not afraid to reveal her beliefs. There was an openness and honesty in the White House that had not been felt for years.

Press Secretary Sheila Weidenfeld was overwhelmed with the response when Betty made public her views on ERA, abortion, and premarital sex. In a 1975 "60 Minutes" segment, Betty admitted she

© 1974 by NEA, Inc.

"Just think, dear! Somewhere out there Rich Little is having a terrible time trying to impersonate you!"

would not be surprised if daughter Susan told her she was having an affair. Mail was emormous both supporting and opposing her remarks.

Betty visited China, where she danced with students, Russia, Europe, and Japan. She spent hours visiting children's hospitals. She was also a volunteer for No Greater Love, an organization that helps families of dead or missing servicemen. She showed poise and control under fire when a speaker on the platform she was sharing collapsed and later died of a heart attack. While the doctors, paramedics, and Secret Service worked in the background, Betty calmly and quietly asked the audience to bow their heads and pray for the health of the victim, Rabbi Dr. Maurice Sage.

In 1974, Betty had a cancerous right breast removed. This spurred hundreds of other women to go in for examinations. Within weeks of Betty's operation, Marguerite (Happy) Rockefeller, wife of the vice-president, had one of her breasts removed and credited Betty with saving her life.

The Secret Service nicknamed her Pinafore and she instituted an open friendship with the White House staff. No longer were servants afraid to say hello to the presidential family. Mischevious Betty had a running game with the cleaning staff. Near the Oval Office was a statue of a winged woman with a large bowl on her head. Originally there had been a scroll in her outstretched hand, but it had been lost. Betty loved to place a cigarette in its place.

Betty also made two noted television appearances during her tenure as First Lady, both on CBS. She appeared on the "Mary Tyler Moore" sitcom as herself. In the episode, Mary's boss, Lou Grant (played by Ed Asner), hosted a party which Mary avoided because she thought it would be boring. Both the president and Mrs. Ford did attend, but Ford mislaid his pipe. Betty called Lou asking if he had found the pipe. Mary did not believe it was really Betty calling, so Lou put Mary on the phone. The dialogue which followed was humorous: "Hello Mary, this is Betty, Betty Ford." "Hello Betty, this is Mary, Queen of Scots." Betty's other TV appearance was in the final segment of "Bicentennial Minute" on July 4, 1976. CBS had been running daily synopses of events that had occurred 200 years ago. The network wanted Ford to appear on the final segment, but because of fair campaign laws and cries from the Democrats, the First Lady appeared instead.

Many believe Betty was an issue during the 1976 presidential campaign because of her outspoken views, especially on abortion and the ERA. More often than not, campaign signs read "Betty's Husband for President" or "Keep Betty in the White House." Ford lost in a very close election to Jimmy Carter. Betty and many others felt that, had the election been one week later, Ford could have won.

Post White House: Upon leaving the White House, the Fords retired to Palm Springs, California, in hopes the drier air would help Betty's arthritis. In 1977, the entire family confronted Betty on her drug and alcohol problem. In a heartbreaking session, they told her she was slowly killing herself. The problem started in 1964, when a doctor prescribed pain pills after Betty suffered a pinched nerve in her neck. Since that time, she had become addicted to the pills. Even eighteen months with a psychiatrist did not help Betty rid herself the addiction.

She was admitted to Long Beach Naval Hospital's Alcohol and Drug Rehabilitation Service Center. While there, she also admitted a dependency on alcohol. She also learned that she should start doing things for Betty and not Betty's husband. Going public with the problem drew almost as many letters of support as when she was in the White House. Plans were soon unveiled for the Betty Ford Drug Treatment Center, which opened in 1982 as part of the Eisenhower Medical Center. Many people, including celebrities, have been helped at the center.

Betty has written two books, *The Times of My Life,* 1978, and *Betty: A Glad Awakening,* 1982.

Honors/Honorary Degrees
University of Michigan, 1976
Boards
The Betty Ford Center
National Arthritis Foundation
League of Republican Women
Eisenhower Medical Center
Nursing Home Advisory Committee
National Symphony Orchestra

ELEANOR ROSALYNN SMITH CARTER

(1927–)

First Lady (1977–1981)

The Straight Facts

Born: August 18, 1927
Birthplace: Plains, Georgia
Ancestry: English
Physical Characteristics: 5'7" tall, auburn hair, brown eyes
Religion: Methodist, then Baptist
Husband: James Earl Carter (1924–)
Date of Marriage: July 7, 1946
Place of Marriage: Plains, Georgia

Children: Three sons, one daughter
Firsts: To attend cabinet meetings
White House Portrait: George Augusta, ground floor corridor

The More Colorful Facts

Astrological Sign: Leo
Nicknames: Steel Magnolia, Iron Lady, Sister Rosalynn
Childhood and Family Life: Rosalynn (pronounced Rose-Lynn) is the oldest of four children of auto mechanic Wilburn Edgar Smith and Frances Alletta (Allie) Murray, a seamstress. She was named for her maternal grandmother. Her father died when she was a teenager, and Rosalynn helped her mother with the housework and worked in a beauty parlor. She was valedictorian of the Class of 1944 at Plains High School and briefly attended Georgia Southwestern College where she was sophomore class vice-president. Her family was deeply religious, and she often attended Sunday services with various relatives at the Lutheran, Methodist, and Baptist church. Her family was Republican and she once visited the White House at age six. As a child she was known as neat in person and work and always had the largest hair bow of any girl in her class.
Courtship and Marriage: A high-school friend was Ruth Carter, whose older brother, James Earl (Jimmy), was attending Annapolis Naval Academy. In a typical small town environment, everyone knew everyone else, but Rosalynn did not really know Jimmy. She fell in love with his picture before she fell in love with him. Ruth and Rosalynn spent many evenings creating a fantasy romance between Rosalynn and Carter. When he came home on leave, Ruth arranged for the two to meet. Before his leave was up, he told his mother that he was going to marry Rosalynn someday.

He proposed during the Christmas 1945 break but she turned him down. Six weeks later, at the Washington Birthday Ball, he proposed again and she accepted. One of the first gifts he gave her was a compact with the Carter family motto ILYTG (I Love You The Goodest) on the lid. The second was a book entitled *The Navy Wife.*

They were married following his graduation from Annapolis at Plains Methodist Church. The bride was eighteen and dressed in an afternoon dress with a halo hat. The groom was twenty-two and wore his dress whites. There were no attendants and no invitations; whoever wanted to come, came. They honeymooned in Chimney Rock, North Carolina.
Children: The Carters have four children. John, known as Jack (1947–), is

an attorney. James Earl III, known as Chip (1950–), is an accountant. Donnel Jeffrey, known as Jeff (1952–), owns a computer software company. Only daughter Amy (1970–) is now working in a factory that casts bronze statues and is a political activist.

Personal Notes: Rosalynn is a good dancer (her Secret Service code name was Dancer), who loves to garden and cook. She knits, sews most of her own clothes, and loves to read. She enjoys classical music, theatre, Robert Redford movies, and Willie Nelson tunes. When Amy took violin lessons at the White House, Rosalynn did too. She reads the Bible daily, sometimes in Spanish. She enjoys tennis, golf, fishing, and jogging with her husband. She suffers from severe allergies and wears contact lenses.

Naval Wife: For seven years after their marriage, Rosalynn followed Carter from base to base. They lived in Norfolk, Virgina; San Diego, California; Oahu, Hawaii; and New Haven, Connecticut. She ran the household, handled finances, and raised the children while Carter was at sea. As a young bride, the only things she could cook were breakfast, brownies, and chocolate fudge. The first real argument they ever had was when Carter announced he was leaving the navy to return home to run the family peanut business after his father's death.

Politician's Wife: In the first years after leaving the navy, the Carters ran the peanut business together; Rosalynn kept the books. They lived in a $31-per-month federal housing project and in the first year made a profit of $254. Rosalynn taught Sunday school and was active in the PTA and the local garden club. When Jimmy won a Georgia state senate seat in 1962, she was an active participant in the campaign. She made calls, shook hands, and clipped newspaper articles for his attention. Amusing stories have been told of Rosalynn's learning early in the game to go back and pick up discarded campaign literature and of the man who shook her hand so hard that her earring fell off. She made campaign appearances in unusual places such as in a hot-air balloon, at an auto auction, during rattlesnake roundup, and at a chicken-processing plant. She also claims to have been thrown out of or ordered away from every K Mart in Georgia because the chain does not allow soliciting in front of their premises.

While Carter was serving as governor of Georgia, she kept the books, supervised the staff, which included some prison trustees, and published a book on the governor's mansion. Proceeds from the sale of the book were used to improve the gardens of the home. She became involved in causes, especially mental health and the elderly. She was appointed a member of the Governor's Commission to Improve Services for the Mentally and Emotionally Handicapped and visited every mental health facility in the state. She served as honorary chairperson of the state's Special Olympics. She also worked as a volunteer worker at a local hospital.

The Carters entertained a great deal, and Rosalynn had as many as 800 guests per week for dinner. They served only wine and no hard liquor in the governor's mansion. According to Georgia law, Carter could not succeed himself so he announced to his family that he was going to run for president. "President of what?" was their reply.

During the 1976 campaign the Carters were definite underdogs who campaigned for two years before the convention. Rosalynn served as campaign advisor, wrote and delivered speeches, and helped make staff decisions. Carter called her his secret weapon during the campaign. Because of her soft Southern drawl, Rosalynn often had trouble getting her message across to Northerners. She quickly learned she was "Mrs. Cahtah" and not "Mrs. Carter." When her luggage, including her best wig, were stolen, she wore the same outfit for days in a row, washing it out nightly in the sink in her hotel room.

The entire family was involved in the campaign and at times Rosalynn was embarrassed by them. There was her beer-drinking, blunt brother-in-law, Billy, and Amy and her lemonade stand. Rosalynn was once mortified to see Henry Kissinger at a briefing drinking lemonade in a Tweety Bird glass he had bought at Amy's lemonade stand.

First Lady: The Carters were the first family to walk the 1½ miles back to the White House after the inauguration ceremony. Rosalynn wore the same blue chiffon dress as she had worn to Carter's inauguration as governor. Like Charlie Taft, Amy brought a book along so she wouldn't be bored during the many events. Hers was titled *The Mixed-Up Files of Mrs. Basile E. Frankweiler*. Inauguration day was also the first time the president and his wife had seen the White House living quarters. Rosalynn picked out the Thaddeus Stevens School for Amy to attend, the first public school for a presidential child since 1906.

As First Lady, Rosalynn continued to espouse her main causes of mental health, the elderly, the ERA, and Jimmy Carter. She attended cabinet meetings and had working lunches with the president to discuss issues. She was shocked to receive the food bill for the first ten days of their White House life; it amounted to over $600 because no one told the cook to use leftovers. She also carefully watched the maintenance of the White House by the staff. She once caught a maid dancing around the room just making an appearance of cleaning. Rosalynn often left a cracker on a table; if it was gone, she knew the staff had cleaned.

Entertaining was done with the help of Social Secretary Gretchen Poston and Press Secretary Mary Finch Hoyt. Highlights included dinners for President Anwar Sadat of Egypt and Prime Minister Menacham Begin of Israel, Soviet premier Leonid Brezhnev, and Chinese vice-chairman Deng Xiaoping.

She traveled across the country visiting hospitals and mental-health facilities and advocated the passing of the Equal Rights Amendment. She was Carter's envoy to Cambodian refugee camps, took a tour to Central and South America, met the Pope in Rome, and attended the inauguration of President José Lopez Portillo of Mexico.

During the Iran hostage crisis, the Carters felt as if they were hostages, too. When Carter was defeated for re-election in 1980, Rosalynn was more hurt and bitter than he was.

Post White House: Rosalynn continues to be involved in special causes. She has participated in the Habitat for Humanity housing campaign and the Friendship Force, a group promoting friendship around the world. She attended ceremonies dedicating the Jimmy Carter Presidential Center in Atlanta, Georgia, where she keeps an office. She wrote her autobiography, *First Lady From Plains* in 1984 and *Everything to Gain: Making the Most of the Rest of Your Life* with Carter in 1987, a project she says she will never undertake again.

Honors/Honorary Degrees

Honorary Chairman, Georgia Special Olympics, 1971–1975

University of Notre Dame, 1987

Volunteer of the Year, Southwestern Association of Volunteer Services, 1976

Vincent DeFrancis Outstanding Service to Humanity, American Humane Association, 1979

Volunteer of the Decade, National Mental Health Association, 1980

Morehouse College, 1980

Presidential Citation, American Psychology Association, 1982

Distinguished Christian Woman's Award, Southern Baptist Theological Seminary, 1984

Nathan S. Kline Medal of Merit, International Committee Against Mental Mental Illness, 1984

Honorary Fellow, American Psychiatric Association

Winthrop College, 1984

Wesleyan College, 1986

Boards

Georgia Governor's Commission to Improve Services for the Mentally and Emotionally Handicapped, 1971

President's Commission for Mental Health, 1977–1978

Honorary Chair, John F. Kennedy Center for Performing Arts, 1977–1980

Member Emeritus, National Association of Mental Health
The Friendship Force
The Gannett Company
Crested Butte Physically Challenged Ski Program
Habitat for Humanity
Trustee, The Menninger Foundation
Sponsor, The National Alliance for Research on Schizophrenia and
Depression

ANNE FRANCES (NANCY) ROBBINS DAVIS REAGAN

(1923–)

First Lady (1981–1989)

The Straight Facts

Born: July 6, 1921
Birthplace: New York, New York
Ancestry: English
Physical Characteristics: 5'4" tall, brown hair, hazel eyes
Religion: Presbyterian
Husband: Ronald Wilson Reagan (1911–)
Date of Marriage: March 4, 1952
Place of Marriage: North Hollywood, California

Children: One son, one daughter
Firsts: To sing on the Broadway stage
To speak at the United Nations
To be adopted
White House Portrait: Aaron Shikler (not yet displayed)

The More Colorful Facts

Astrological Sign: Cancer
Nicknames: Nancy, Cuddles, First Mannequin, Fancy Nancy
Childhood and Family Life: Anne Frances Robbins is the daughter of salesman/playboy Kenneth Robbins and actress Edith Luckett. She was named for a paternal ancestor, Sister Anne Ayers, the first American Episcopal nun; her mother always called her Nancy. Her parents divorced when she was a baby. While Edith traveled with shows, Nancy was raised by an aunt and uncle, Virginia and Audley Galbraith, in Baltimore, and attended Sidwell Friends School. Once Edith took Nancy and cousin Charlotte Galbraith to the White House for the annual Easter Egg Roll. When Nancy was eight, Edith married Dr. Loyal Davis of Chicago. He adopted her when she was fourteen and sent her to Girls Latin School, Camp Ketchewa, and Smith College. She made her debut in 1939 at Chicago's Casino Club.
Actress: It seemed natural for Nancy to follow in her mother's footsteps. Her godmother was the legendary actress Alla Nazimova. Broadway, radio, and Hollywood stars were frequent visitors at the Davis home. Her first leading role was as a senior at Girl's Latin in George S. Kaufman's *The First Lady.* Upon her graduation from Smith, she joined family friend Zasu Pitts's road company and formally launched her career as an actress. She worked on and off Broadway, toured with traveling companies, and did modeling. She dated regularly and enjoyed going to New York's famed Stork Club with such luminaries as Clark Gable and Walter Winchell. She often snitched rolls from the table to take home, thinking no one would see her. The owner finally sent over a stick of butter to go with her rolls and that ended her pilfering.

It was Benny Thau, vice-president of Metro-Goldwyn-Mayer, who suggested she go to Hollywood for a screen test. She "read" her part against Howard Keel and was directed by George Cukor. She became a contract player and shaved two years off her age in her studio biography.
Courtship and Marriage: In the midst of the Red scare in Hollywood, Nancy began to receive Communist Party propaganda. She consulted with director Mervyn LeRoy who promised to talk to Screen Actors Guild

president Ronald Reagan on her behalf. She had earlier met Reagan at a 1949 dinner at the home of producer Dore Schary. Reagan found there were five actresses named Nancy Davis and told LeRoy that the Screen Actors Guild would stand behind her. She wanted to hear it from Reagan himself and they arranged to meet for an early dinner. They went to LaRue's, then to Ciro's night club to hear Sophie Tucker. They dated for several years before marrying at the Little Brown Church in North Hollywood. Fellow actor William Holden served as best man for the forty-one-year-old groom, and Holden's wife, Ardis (actress Brenda Marshall) stood up for the thirty-one-year-old bride. The couple honeymooned at the Mission Inn, Riverside, California, and Phoenix.

Children: The Reagans have two children. Patricia Anne (1952–), known professionally as Patti Davis, is an actress/songwriter. She married yoga instructor Paul Grilley in 1983. Ronald Prescott (1958–) was called Skipper as a child and is a dancer/actor/newsman. He married researcher Doria Palmieri in 1980.

Personal Notes: Nancy is a good politician with savvy and flair. She loves flowers, fine clothes, and Chinese urns. She enjoys reading cookbooks but not cooking. She has a good sense of humor and calls herself a frustrated interior decorator. She deals with frustration sitting in a warm bath and having imaginary conversations with the person who caused her pain.

Politician's Wife: When Reagan announced he was running for governor of California in 1966, Nancy was all for it. Dr. Loyal Davis was a staunch ultraconservative and passed on this philosophy to his adopted daughter. An active member of Reagan's advisory staff, Nancy shook hands, supervised schedules, gave advice, and watched adoringly as Reagan gave speeches. Friend and foe alike have called that look "The Gaze." She participated in question-and-answer periods but made no speeches on her own.

They lived in the governor's mansion in Sacramento for only four months. Nancy found it a decaying firetrap and refused to raise her children there. At their own expense, the Reagans rented a $1,500-a-month home on 48th Street in a fashionable part of town. To justify her decision, she took wives of state leaders through the old mansion until funds were raised to renovate and refurbish it.

She was a good political wife, decorating offices and attending teas, luncheons, brunches, and receptions. She christened a minisub, the SS *Roughneck*, but only after five swings of the champagne bottle. She became interested in the Foster Grandparents Program, which linked senior citizens with mentally and physically handicapped children. She was also active in the POW-MIA cause during the Vietnam

War and wrote a column for their organization's newsletter. She visited veterans' hospitals and wrote letters to veterans' families.

Despite her volunteer work Nancy was often criticized for any activities she did with her wealthy friends. Critics claimed Nancy and the "Girls," who included Betsy Bloomingdale, Bonita Granville, Mary Jane Wick, Lee Annenberg, and Jane Dart cared only for fine fashions and themselves. In truth, they donated much time and money to charitable causes.

When Reagan declared for president in 1976, Nancy was not in favor of his entering the race. She knew he had little time to prepare, no chance of taking the nomination away from Gerald Ford, and she felt it was a bad decision. It was the last major political decision he made without consulting her. At the convention, she thought he should have withdrawn before the ballots were counted. Nancy felt offended because First Lady Betty Ford arrived at the same time she did, drowning the applause for Nancy.

After leaving the governor's office, the Reagans returned to Pacific Palisades and their home at 1669 San Onafre Drive. They also frequently went to Rancho del Cielo, their ranch in the Santa Ynez Mountains. It was here that they celebrated their twenty-fifth wedding anniversary. Their present to each other was a canoe named *Tru Love*. They began to plan for 1980 and another run for the presidency.

This time they were ready. Again, Nancy was an integral part of the team, choosing advisors, and making a few speeches. During the campaign she regularly "bowled" an orange down the aisle of their campaign plane, called "Leadership 1980." She also made a habit of passing chocolates to each reporter on the plane. She was not in favor of offering the vice-presidency to Gerald Ford. Nancy basked in Reagan's glory on nomination night and had a near mishap when she fell in her private box.

First Lady: Both the start and finish of Nancy's tenure as First Lady were shaky. The problems started at the "Million Dollar Inaugural," so called because of the onslaught of wealthy people who converged on Washington. The Reagan years brought the return of white tie and tails, long formal gowns, glittering jewels, and Hollywood celebrities. The impression was given that only the socially elite mattered.

New occupants to the White House are given $50,000 by Congress to redo the Family Quarters to their liking. Nancy decided that wasn't enough, and with $822,641 donated by friends (tax deductible), she furnished the rooms to her liking. These same friends also donated $209,888 for the controversial new red china, all within the Reagan's first sixty days in office. The country was soon to learn that red was Nancy's favorite color.

The attempted assassination of Reagan curtailed entertaining for a few months. Vice-President and Mrs. George Bush pinch-hit where possible. Reagan felt his first foreign trip as president should not be a social affair, so he sent his wife as the country's official representative to the wedding of Britain's Prince Charles and Lady Diana Spencer. On *Executive Foxtrot One,* Nancy, ten Secret Service agents, thirteen aides, twenty-two dresses, her hairdresser, and Betsy Bloomingdale flew to London.

The British press did not treat Nancy any more kindly than their American counterparts. They criticized her arrival at a polo match in a six-car convoy protected by Secret Service agents in an armour-plated limosine.Ten minutes later, the queen arrived driving herself and King Constantine of Greece in a station wagon with only two followup vehicles, followed by Princess Anne who arrived driving her own jeep. Nancy was able to convince Stueben to sell a $75,000 cut glass bowl to the British government for $8,000 as a gift from the American people. The evening of the polo match, the queen gave a ball for royalty and aristocracy only. Nancy and Betsy were invited but not French president François Mitterand.

Nancy also ran into criticism when it was revealed that much of her clothing was not owned but given or loaned by her favorite designers Adolfo, Bill Blass, Galanos, and Gucci. She even had her own dresser at I. Magnin's—Miss Donahue. The same was true of her jewelry. Then there were problems when housewives wrote asking for her favorite recipes. They were sent lobster recipes. Quickly realizing the average American cannot afford to cook lobster at home, she substituted macaroni and cheese.

White House Press Corps Chief Helen Thomas advised Nancy to find a cause to take criticism away from herself. She again chose to promote the idea of foster grandparents. In 1981, she co-authored a book on the subject and convinced old friend Frank Sinatra to record the theme song for the campaign. She also took an active role in the Just Say No to Drugs campaign. She made numerous television, radio, and lecture appearances. She appeared in a PBS televison special "The Chemical People" and on NBC's "Diff'rent Strokes." In 1985, she hosted a conference on drug abuse for First Ladies from around the world.

Press relations improved a little when she appeared at the 1982 Press Club Gridiron Dinner. Dressed in a bag lady outfit, she sang to the tune of "Second Hand Rose," a song called "Second Hand Clothes." She also smashed a plate which resembled her controversial china.

The 1985 inauguration was the coldest on record. The entire ceremony was moved indoors and the parade postponed until summer. The Reagans agreed to appear at a rally for all the high school students who could not march. After making a brief speech, Nancy sat down. Seconds later she jumped up aghast, saying, "I forgot to introduce my roommate." The whole crowd, including Reagan, roared with laughter. During the second term she had a mastectomy and several cancerous growths removed from her face, a result of too much California sun.

She has been called the First Lady with too much power. Nancy has been blamed for the dismissal or resignation of several key Reagan aides, including Alexander Haig, Donald Regan, and Lyn Nofziger. Reagan is hard of hearing and wears an aid in one ear, and Nancy has often been caught whispering responses in his ear. This made it appear as if she was making decisions and putting words in his mouth. The Reagans were the first couple to serve two full terms in nearly thirty years. Nancy's advice to future First Ladies is to be yourself, do what interests you, and don't be afraid.

Post White House: The Reagans returned to California to a home built for them by friends at 668 St. Cloud in Bel Air. Nancy continues to be involved in fighting drug addiction. She went on a much publicized drug raid at a crack house. Her autobiography, *My Turn*, was published in October 1989. She was elected to the Board of Directors of the Revlon Corporation in April 1989.

Honors/Honorary Degrees:

    Pepperdine University, 1983

    Georgetown University, 1987

    Woman of the Year, Los Angeles *Times,* 1977

    Permanent Member, Hall of Fame of Ten Best Women in U.S.

    Humanitarian Award, American Camping Association

    Humanitarian Award, National Council on Alcoholism

    Humanitarian Award, United Cerebral Palsy Association

    Humanitarian Award, International Center for the Disabled

    Humanitarian Award, Boys' Town Father Flanagan Award

    Kiwanis World Service Medal, 1986

    Lifetime Award, Variety Clubs International

    Silver Buffalo Award, Boy Scouts of America

Boards

    Honorary National Chair, Aid to Adoption of Special Kids, 1977

    Honorary National Chair, Just Say No Foundation

THE PLAYS OF NANCY DAVIS:

Ramshackle Inn

Cordelia

Lute Song

The Late Christopher Bean

Broken Dishes

THE FILMS OF NANCY DAVIS (REAGAN):

The Doctor and the Girl 1949 Marlette

East Side, West Side 1949 Helen Lee

Shadow on the Wall 1950 Dr. Caroline Canford

The Next Voice You Hear 1950 Mrs. Joe Smith

Night Into Morning 1951 Katherine Mead

It's A Big Country 1952 Miss Coleman

Shadow In the Sky 1952 Betty

Talk About A Stranger 1952 Marge Fontaine

Donovan's Brain 1953 Janice Corey

Hellcats of the Navy* 1957 Helen Blair

Crash Landing 1958 Helen Williams

*The only movie costarring her husband Ronald Reagan.

BARBARA PIERCE BUSH

(1924–)

First Lady (1989–)

The Straight Facts

Born: June 8, 1924
Birthplace: Rye, New York
Ancestry: English
Physical Characteristics: Brown hair, gray eyes
Religion: Episcopalian
Husband: George Herbert Walker Bush (1924–)
Date of Marriage: January 6, 1945
Place of Marriage: Rye, New York
Children: Four sons, two daughters

The More Colorful Facts

Astrological Sign: Gemini

Nicknames: Bar, Silver Fox

Childhood and Family Life: Barbara is the third of four children of *McCalls-/Redbook* magazine publisher Marvin Pierce and Pauline Robinson. She attended Ashley Hall in South Carolina and, briefly, Smith College. Her father would often bring home *McCalls* clothing patterns and Barbara and her friends would use them for paper dolls.

Courtship and Marriage: At a Christmas 1941 dance, she met Andover senior George Bush. The two were introduced by Jack Wozencraft. As Bush didn't waltz, they sat and talked "and haven't stopped since." They became secretly engaged in August 1943, a secret that Bush claimed was kept only from the German and Japanese high command. She continued her schooling while he served as a pilot in the South Pacific during World War II. All his planes were named "Barbara." Barbara married "the first man I ever kissed" in January 1945 at the First Presbyterian Church in Rye. After the war, they were two of forty people that lived in one of Yale University's married housing units. When Bush graduated, they headed for Texas and a career in the oil industry.

Children: The Bushes have six children. George (1946–), John, called Jeb (1953–), Neil (1955–), Marvin (1956–), and Dorothy (1959–). All served as delegates to the 1988 Republican Convention and cast their ballots for their father. Daughter Robin (1949–1953) died of leukemia, after which Barbara's hair turned prematurely white.

Personal Notes: Barbara is an avid gardener who loves tacos, Chinese food, mystery novels, and needlecraft. To stay in shape, she plays doubles in tennis, rides an exercise bike, and walks the family dog. She taught Sunday school and served as a den mother, and in the PTA. She keeps scrapbooks, which now number over sixty, of the family's life and travels.

Politician's Wife: In forty-four years of marriage, Barbara has followed her husband to twenty-nine homes. On the way, she has developed from a shy housewife, terrified of speaking in public, to a seasoned politician. She has been the biggest supporter of Bush's life, career, and causes. The Secret Service nickname for her as "Second Lady" was Tranquility, for the effect she has on Bush. She adopted a few causes of her own. Since Robin's death, she has regularly visited hospitals and befriended patients. When son Neil was discovered to have dyslexia, she became an advocate of illiteracy. She "ghost" wrote an insiders' book on Washington with her dog, C. Fred Bush, with all the proceeds going toward literacy efforts.

I, GEORGE HERBERT WALKER BUSH, DO

I, GEORGE HERBERT WALKER BUSH, DO

READ MY LIPS...

READ MY LIPS...

First Lady: As First Lady, she will continue to support literacy, the fight against AIDS, cancer research, the homeless, and George Bush. Her fashion sense has appealed to a different constituency than that of her predecessor as she does her own hair and refuses to dye it, wears three-strand faux pearls, wears her wrinkles with pride, and acknowledges that she is a size 14. The first six months of her tenure were marked with two events. It was discovered that she was suffering from Graves Disease, a thyroid disorder. In March 1989, First Dog Millie, a springer spaniel, gave birth to six pups, displacing the proud president from his bedroom.

Honors/Honorary Degrees

Stritch College, 1981
Mt. Vernon College, 1981
Hood College, 1983
Howard University, 1987
Distinguished Leadership, United Negro College Fund, 1986
Distinguished American Woman, College of Mt. St. Joseph, 1987

Boards

Reading is Fundamental, Business Council for Effective Literacy
Social Board of Memorial Sloan-Kettering Cancer Center
Children's Oncology Services of Metropolitan Washington
The Kingsbury Center
Literacy Volunteers of the National School Voluntary Program
Laubach Literacy International
Leukemia Society of America
Morehouse School of Medicine
National Organ Donor Awareness Week, 1982–1986

WIVES

Eight wives of the presidents did not serve as First Lady. Five died before their husbands were inaugurated. Two married their husbands after his term of office was completed. One divorced her husband before he became president.

MARTHA WAYLES SKELTON JEFFERSON
(1748–1782)

The Straight Facts

Born: October 30, 1748
Birthplace: Charles City County, Virginia
Ancestry: English
Physical Characteristics: 5'5" tall, auburn hair, brown eyes
Religion: Episcopalian
Husbands: (1) Bathurst Skelton (?-1768)
           (2) Thomas Jefferson (1743–1826)
Date of Marriages: (1) November 20, 1766
                  (2) January 1, 1772
Place of Marriages: (1) Williamsburg, Virginia
                 (2) Williamsburg, Virginia
Children: (1) One son
          (2) One son, five daughters
Died: September 6, 1782
Place of Death: Monticello, Virginia
Burial Place: Monticello, Virginia

The More Colorful Facts

Astrological Sign: Scorpio
Childhhood and Family Life: Not much is known about her early childhood. She was the daughter of John Wayles, a planter and lawyer, and Martha Eppes, the first of his three wives. She had a half-sister, Sally Hemings, the daughter of John Wayles and his slave Elizabeth Hemings. She was educated at home by tutors and visiting guests.
Personal Notes: She was well educated and a constant reader. Her voice was pleasant and she played both the pianoforte and harpsichord. No known portrait of her exists but she was said to have been of slightly above medium-height, with brown eyes and auburn hair, and very beautiful.
First Husband: Martha married first at age eighteen to Bathurst Skelton, a

planter who died less than twenty-two months later. Skelton was the youngest brother of her second stepmother's first husband. She had one son, John who died two years after his father.

Courtship and Marriage: It is thought Martha met her second husband, Thomas Jefferson, in Williamsburg. Family legend has it that he won out over other suitors of the young widow because of their joint love of music and books. She played the harpsichord; he played the violin. During their courtship they read Laurence Sterne's *The Life and Opinions of Tristram Shandy,* a favorite comedy novel of the day. They applied for a license in Williamsburg on December 23, 1771, and were married on New Year's Day, 1772, at her father's home, The Forest. He was twenty-nine and she was twenty-four. After a two-week honeymoon, they set out for Monticello and ran into a horrible snowstorm. Abandoning their carriage, they finished the trip on horseback, arriving late at night to an unheated home because the servants had retired for the night. By all reports, the marriage was one of "uncheckered happiness."

Children: By Jefferson, she had one son and five daughters. Only two girls lived to adulthood. (See Hostesses)

Politician's Wife: Martha did her share of entertaining while Jefferson served in the House of Burgesses and as governor of Virginia. In 1781, she and the children wore forced to flee Monticello when invading British troops came too close to their home. They fled to another Jefferson estate, Poplar Forest. A tragic victim of the flight was six-month-old Lucy Elizabeth who died a few weeks later. Shortly thereafter, Jefferson resigned from the governorship and promised Martha he would not seek public office again. He did not do so while she was alive.

Death: Seven children in less than fourteen years took their toll on Martha's fragile constitution. Less than four months after giving birth to her last child, another Lucy Elizabeth, she died at age thirty-four of complications related to the birth. At her bedside almost constantly for the last two weeks of her illness, Jefferson promised never to marry again. He was inconsolable after her death, refusing to leave his room for three weeks after the funeral. When he did recover, he spent countless hours riding his horse around his estate. For her tombstone, in Greek, Jefferson wrote:

> If in the melancholy shades below,
> The flames of friends and lovers cease to glow,
> Yet mine shall sacred last; mine undecayed,
> Burn on through death and animate my shade.

RACHEL DONELSON ROBARDS JACKSON
(?1767-1828)

The Straight Facts

Born: June 17, 1767(?)
Birthplace: Halifax County, Virginia
Ancestry: English
Physical Characteristics: Black hair, dark brown eyes
Religion: Presbyterian
Husband: (1) Lewis Robards (?1765–1793)
         (2) Andrew Jackson (1767–1845)
Date of Marriages: (1) March 1, 1785
                (2) August 18, 1791 (?); January 17, 1794
Place of Marriages: (1) Harrodsburg, Kentucky
              (2) Natchez, Mississippi; Nashville, Tennessee
Children: One adopted son
Died: December 22, 1828

Place of Death: Nashville, Tennessee
Burial Place: The Hermitage, Nashville, Tennessee
Firsts: Divorcée to marry a president
To smoke tobacco products
White House Portrait: Howard Chandler Christy, East Wing Reception Room

The More Colorful Facts

Astrological Sign: Gemini
Nicknames: Aunt Rachel
Childhood and Family Life: Rachel Donelson was the daughter of iron master/surveyor Colonel John Donelson and Rachel Stockley. There were twelve children in the family and Rachel was the fourth daughter. She had little formal education and was basically illiterate. In her few surviving letters, she spelled her name "Rawchel." When Rachel was twelve, Colonel Donelson led the family and a group of other settlers on a perilous six-month journey from Virginia to Kentucky. (Theodore Roosevelt told part of their story in his book, *The Winning of the West.*) Four years later, the Colonel was killed by Indians, and the family opened a roadhouse to support themselves in Harrodsburg, Kentucky.
First Husband: Captain Lewis Robards, a Revolutionary War hero, was temperamental, flamboyant, and moody. He was a frequent visitor at the Donelson's tavern and was quite taken with the young Rachel. They became engaged and married shortly after they met. The couple lived with his family (ancestors of actor Jason Robards). An unreasonably jealous man, Robards would publicly chastise Rachel for talking to other men. Young Peyton Short had a crush on Rachel and wrote her a love letter that was never delivered. Robards found the letter, accused the unsuspecting Rachel, and challenged Short to a duel. After accepting a $1,000-settlement and a promise that Short would leave town, the duel was called off. Robards sent for Rachel's brother Samuel Donelson to take her back to her family saying, "she did not behave with the discretion he had the right to expect." Both sides of the family blamed Robard's jealousies and not Rachel for the problems.
Courtship and Marriage: Back in Harrodsburg, Rachel again worked at the family roadhouse, where young lawyer Andrew Jackson was boarding. Instantly attracted to her, he respected Rachel's married state. The Robards reconciled but separated again. In 1790, Robards petitioned the Virginia legislature (Kentucky still being part of the Virginia territory) for an Enabling Act, the right to be heard before a judge and jury and to

sue for divorce. To hide her shame, Rachel went south to stay with relatives.

Jackson and Rachel corresponded and, assuming the bill of divorce had been passed, were married at the Natchez home of her uncle, Colonel Thomas Marston Green, Jr. There is some controversy as to the date of the wedding. It is believed to have taken place in 1791, but an uncle's will, dated 1789, leaves part of his estate to Rachel Donelson, wife of Judge Andrew Jackson. The latter date seems improbable because she was still living with Robards in 1789. In December 1793, they learned that on September 27, 1793, the Virginia legislature had finally passed the divorce decree. Incensed, Jackson, who was known for his temper, wanted to kill Robards. And, he blamed himself, a lawyer, for not making sure the divorce was final. Despite his protests that their marriage was legal and Rachel was innocent, friends persuaded them to marry again to dispel any claims of an illegal marriage. This second ceremony was performed in January 1794 by the Rev. Thomas Craighead in Nashville. Nevertheless, Rachel would spend the rest of her life labeled an adulteress and a bigamist.

Children: Rachel suffered several miscarriages and could have no children of her own. They adopted one of her brother Severn's twin sons and named him Andrew Jackson, Jr. (1809–1865). They also adopted an Indian baby named Lincoyer, whom Jackson had found after a battle during the Seminole War. He died at age sixteen of tuberculosis.

Personal Notes: In her younger days, Rachel was a good dancer, a great storyteller, and an excellent horsewoman. But, later, tarnished by the slander of adultry, she did not socialize much; she often flinched when meeting strangers. Growing older, she became quite portly and preferred to stay at home, gardening or reading her Bible. She was baptized by the Rev. Gideon Blackburn in 1816 and was a devoted Presbyterian for the rest of her life. Jackson built a church for her on the grounds of their Hermitage home so she would have a formal place of worship. She owned a parrot named Poor Poll and smoked cigars and pipes.

Soldier's Wife: While Jackson fought in the War of 1812, she stayed home running their first farm, Hunter's Hill. She had a miniature of herself painted for him to wear on a black cord around his neck while they were separated, and he wore it for the rest of his life. Rachel traveled south to join her victorious husband after the Battle of New Orleans. One of the matrons of society, a Mrs. Livingston, took Rachel under her wing, choosing her costumes, jewelry, and teaching her how to act in society. For once, Rachel was happy, as no one knew of her past. She gained the confidence to appear in public with Jackson.

Politician's Wife: Rachel accompanied Jackson to Florida when he became territorial minister in 1821. She also went with him to Washington and Tennessee's capital. Mostly, however, she stayed at home and ran the new farm, called the Hermitage. She became a very good manager. Jackson's runs for the presidency again brought up the scandal of their marriage. She supported his decision to run but said, "I'd rather be a doorkeeper in the house of God than live in that palace in Washington."

Death: Following Jackson's election as president in 1828, Rachel made plans for the journey to Washington. While shopping for her inaugural gown, she overheard gossips talking about her adultery and backwoods ways. She collapsed when she realized that Jackson had been hiding such maliciousness from her. Returning home, she suffered a heart attack. Five days later, a second attack proved fatal. Jackson refused to believe she was dead and ordered doctors to bleed her. Finally realizing that she was gone, he sat holding her hand all night. Her inaugural gown became her burial shroud. Nashville stores closed on the day of the funeral and nearly the entire town turned out. The Rev. William Hume delivered the sermon, conducting the service from Rachel's own church. Jackson picked one of Rachel's favorite garden spots for her tomb and wrote the following for her gravestone:

> Here lie the remains of Mrs. Rachel Jackson
> wife of President Jackson who died the 22nd
> of December, 1828. Age, 61 years. Her face
> was fair, her person pleasing, her temper
> amiable, her heart kind; she delighted in relieving
> the wants of her fellow creatures, and
> cultivated that divine pleasure by the most
> liberal and unpretending methods; to the poor
> she was a benefactor; to the rich an example;
> to the wretched a comforter; to the prosperous
> an ornament; her piety went hand in hand with
> her benevolence and she thanked her creator
> for being permitted to do good. A being so
> gentle and so virtuous slander might wound, but
> could not dishonor. Even death, when he bore her
> from the arms of her husband, could but transport
> her to the bosom of her God.

HANNAH HOES VAN BUREN

(1783–1819)

The Straight Facts

Born: March 8, 1783
Birthplace: Kinderhook, New York
Ancestry: Dutch
Physical Characteristics: Golden-blonde hair, blue eyes
Religion: Dutch Reformed, then Presbyterian
Husband: Martin Van Buren (1782–1862)
Date of Marriage: February 21, 1807
Place of Marriage: Catskill, New York
Children: Four sons
Died: February 5, 1819
Place of Death: Albany, New York

Burial Place: Kinderhook Cemetery, Kinderhook, New York
Official Portrait: Unknown artist, Columbia County Historical Society, Kinderhook, New York

The More Colorful Facts

Astrological Sign: Pisces
Nicknames: Jannetje (Dutch for Hannah.)
Childhood and Family: Hannah was the daughter of John Dircksen Hoes and Maria Quackenboss. The original family name was Goes. She went to a local school taught by Vrouw Lange.
Courtship and Marriage: Hannah and Martin Van Buren were childhood sweethearts. She was a distant relative of his mother, Maria Hoes Van Alen Van Buren. They were married on February 21, 1807, at the Huxton House, in Catskill, New York, which was owned by her brother-in-law. The ceremony was performed by Judge Moses Cantine. They were married in Catskill instead of Kinderhook, Van Buren's home, for two reasons. First, they only wanted the family to attend. Second, it was a custom for the bridegroom to invite the entire town to the wedding and they wanted to save the expense. Martin was twenty-one and Hannah was twenty.
Children: They had four sons, and one daughter who was stillborn.
Death: Hannah was slow to recover from the birth of her fifth child in 1817. Doctors suspected tuberculosis and ordered complete bed rest. She slowly deteriorated and died a year later at age thirty-six. At her request, the custom of providing scarves for the pallbearers to wear was abandoned and the money set aside to pay for them was used to feed the poor. She was first interred at the Second Presbyterian Church, Albany, but in 1855 was moved to the Kinderhook Cemetery. Van Buren ordered a twenty-foot granite obelisk from Darling and Company of Hudson, New York, to mark her grave. Interestingly, even though Van Buren had said she was the guiding force of his life, she is never mentioned in his 782-page autobiography. Historians believe it is because he advocated the separation of political and private lives.

CAROLINE CARMICHAEL MCINTOSH FILLMORE
(1813–1881)

The Straight Facts

Born: October 21, 1813
Birthplace: Morristown, New Jersey
Ancestry: English
Religion: Baptist
Husbands: (1) Ezekiel C. McIntosh (? – ?)
　　　　　 (2) Millard Fillmore (1800–1874)
Date of Marriages: (1)?
　　　　　　　　　 (2) February 10, 1858
Place of Marriages: (1) Morristown, New Jersey
　　　　　　　　　　 (2) Albany, New York
Children: None
Died: August 11, 1881

Place of Death: Buffalo, New York
Burial Place: Forest Lawn Cemetery, Buffalo, New York

The More Colorful Facts

Astrological Sign: Libra
Childhood and Family Life: Little is known about Caroline's life. She was the daughter of Charles Carmichael, a New Jersey merchant, and Temperance Blachley. She attended finishing school in New York.
First Husband: Caroline's first husband, Ezekiel McIntosh, was one of the builders of the Mohawk and Hudson Railroad.
Courtship and Marriage: After a brief courtship, she married former president Millard Fillmore on February 10, 1858 in the Hamilton Room of the Schuyler Mansion in Albany. The room was so named because Alexander Hamilton married Betsy Schuyler there in 1791. The Fillmores took a long delayed honeymoon to Europe in 1866.
Marriage Terms: Caroline was a wealthy widow at the time of her marriage. The prenuptial contract between her and Fillmore stated that he would assume complete control of her fortune, without any accountability, after the marriage. In the event of her death before his, the entire estate would be turned over to him. In the event of his death before hers, she would only inherit one-third of his money. Although there were many snickers about this contract, those who knew Fillmore well said he would always behave in the most correct manner.
Children: Caroline had no children by either marriage.
Death: After Fillmore's death in 1874, she became senile. Her death seven years later was attritubed to senility. She was buried next to Fillmore and his first wife and daughter in Buffalo. The Rev. Dr. Gordon, pastor of the Washington Street Baptist Church conducted the service. Because of her mental state, the McIntosh family contested the will as they did not want their money going to Fillmore's son.

ELLEN LEWIS HERNDON ARTHUR

(1837–1880)

The Straight Facts

Born: August 30, 1837
Birthplace: Culpeper, Virginia
Ancestry: English
Physical Characteristics: Brown hair, dark eyes, frail build
Religion: Episcopalian
Husband: Chester Alan Arthur (1829–1886)
Date of Marriage: October 25, 1859
Place of Marriage: New York, New York
Children: Two sons, one daughter

Died: January 12, 1880
Place of Death: New York, New York
Burial Place: Rural Cemetery, Albany, New York
Official Portrait: Unknown artist, the Library of Congress

The More Colorful Facts

Astrological Sign: Virgo

Childhood and Family Life: Ellen was the only child of William Lewis Herndon, explorer of the Amazon, and Frances Elizabeth Hansbrough. A monument to Commodore Herndon was erected at Annapolis Naval Academy after he heroically went down with his ship, the SS *Central America* during a storm, after all the women and children were saved. Her aristocratic Virginia ancestry can be traced to seventeenth-century England. A great-great-grandfather was among the first Virginians to muster a regiment during the Revolutionary War. Ellen had a privileged childhood, attending private schools, with private tutors.

Courtship and Marriage: On a trip to New York City with her widowed mother, she met young lawyer Chester Arthur. Arthur was a border at the same hotel as her cousin, medical student Dabney Herndon, who made the introduction. After a brief courtship, he proposed on the porch of the U.S. Hotel in Saratoga Springs. They were married at the Calvary Episcopal Church, two months after her twentieth birthday. The newlyweds returned from a brief honeymoon to live with her mother at 34 W. 25th Street in New York City.

Children: They had three children, two boys and a girl. William Lewis Herndon Arthur died at age two in 1863 of a brain disorder. The doctors told the young couple that it was probably their fault he died as "they tried to fill his young brain with too much knowledge and over-taxed it with intellectual demands." As a result, Chester, Jr. (1864–1937) and Ellen Herndon Arthur Pinkerton (1871–1915) were spoiled and indulged by their parents in their early years.

Personal Life: Ellen was gracious, charming, and said to be quite beautiful. She played the piano and was an accomplished horsewoman. She had a wonderful contralto voice and sang in the church choir and the Mendelssohn Glee Club. She was frequently in demand to perform at charitable events. During their courtship, Arthur and Ellen would often attend musical events and their favorite song was "Robin Adair." She did not get along well with Arthur's family, however. During the Civil War, they made fun of her accent, questioned her as to where her sympathies lay, and referred to her as "Chet's rebel wife."

Politician's Wife: With the onset of the Civil War, Confederate sympathizer Frances Herndon went back to Virginia. Arthur bought a home for his family at 123 Lexington Avenue in New York City. He saw the need to entertain frequently and lavishly. As a genteel daughter of the old South, Ellen was well prepared for the challenge. However, the constant entertaining began to take its toll. Arthur would often stay out all night, began spending more time with political cronies than with his wife and family.

Death: While waiting for her carriage after attending a late night concert, Ellen caught a cold which developed into pneumonia. Arthur was in Albany and, by the time he arrived home, she was unconscious. She died without ever regaining consciousness at age forty-two, ten months before her husband was elected vice-president. The funeral was held at the Church of the Heavenly Rest and burial was at Albany's Rural Cemetery.

Tribute: It was rumored that, prior to her death, Ellen was going to separate from Arthur because he was constantly away from home. When asked about this, his reply was, "I may be president of the United States, but my personal life is my own damned business." Nevertheless, he ordered a bouquet of flowers from the White House conservatory placed before her portrait daily. He also donated a stained-glass window in her memory to St. John's Episcopal Church, which was placed where he could see it from the White House. He never remarried.

MARY SCOTT LORD DIMMICK HARRISON
(1858–1948)

The Straight Facts

Born: April 30, 1858
Birthplace: Honesdale, Pennsylvania
Ancestry: English
Religion: Presbyterian
Husbands: (1) Walter Erskine Dimmick (?-1882)
        (2) Benjamin Harrison (1833–1901)
Date of Marriages: (1) October 22, 1881
        (2) April 6, 1896
Place of Marriages: (1) ?
        (2) New York, New York
Children: (2) One daughter

Died: January 15, 1948
Place of Death: New York, New York
Burial Place: Crown Hill Cemetery, Indianapolis, Indiana
Firsts: Presidential widow who was not a First Lady to be awarded franking privileges by Congress

The More Colorful Facts

Astrological Sign: Taurus
Childhood and Family Life: Mary was the daughter of Russell Farnham Lord, chief engineer, later general manager, of the Delaware and Hudson Canal Company, and Elizabeth Mayhew Scott. Elizabeth was the sister of Caroline Scott Harrison, first wife of Benjamin Harrison.
First Husband: Her first husband was attorney Walter Erskine Dimmick, who died in 1882 after only three months of marriage, leaving her a widow at twenty-four. Returning to Washington, Mary lived with her mother. When her mother died, Mary was invited to live in the White House by her aunt. She assisted her Aunt Caroline in her social affairs and served as her secretary.
Courtship and Marriage: Three years after Caroline's death, Mary became engaged to her uncle, Benjamin Harrison, on Christmas Day, 1895. They were married four months later at St. Thomas Protestant Episcopal Church in New York City. Forty guests were present, but conspicuously absent were the groom's children, who were older than the bride and aghast at the union. The bride was thirty-seven and the groom was sixty-two. They took a delayed honeymoon to Europe in 1899 and built a summer home called Berkeley Lodge (after the Harrison family estate in Virginia) in the Adirondacks.
Children: In 1897, Mary gave birth to a daughter, Elizabeth. The baby was younger than four of her father's grandchildren. Elizabeth (1897–1955) became a successful lawyer and had two children, one of whom married a great-grandson of President James Garfield.
Death: A widow again at forty-three, she lived another forty-six years after Harrison. She is buried in the Harrison family plot in Indianapolis. During World War I, Mary served as chairman of the New York City division of the War Camp Community Service. She was also active in Republican Party affairs.

ALICE HATHAWAY LEE ROOSEVELT
(1861–1884)

The Straight Facts

Born: July 29, 1861
Birthplace: Boston, Massachusetts
Ancestry: English
Physical Characteristics: 5'7" tall, 125 lbs., blonde hair, blue eyes
Religion: Unitarian
Husband: Theodore Roosevelt (1858–1919)
Date of Marriage: October 27, 1880
Place of Marriage: Brookline, Massachusetts
Children: One daughter
Died: February 14, 1884

Place of Death: New York, New York
Burial Place: Greenwood Cemetery, Brookline, Massachusetts

The More Colorful Facts

Astrological Sign: Leo
  Nickname: Little Sunshine
Childhood and Family Life: The second daughter of George Cabot Lee, a Chestnut Hill banker, and Caroline Watts Haskell, Alice went to the finest schools, made her debut in Boston, and toured Europe.
Courtship and Marriage: She met future husband Theodore Roosevelt at the home of cousin Richard Saltonstall. In his diary, Roosevelt wrote ". . . first saw her on 10/28/1878 and loved her as soon as I saw her sweet, fair young face." They courted during 1878 and 1879 and became engaged on January 25, 1880. Ten months later they wed on Roosevelt's twenty-second birthday (she was nineteen). They went on a brief honeymoon to England and Ireland. The newlyweds lived at 55 W. 45th Street, New York City, later moving in with his mother at 6 W. 57th Street.
Children: Alice gave birth to her only child, a namesake daughter, on February 12, 1884. Young Alice, who would become known as "Princess Alice" during her father's presidency, was known for her impulsive ways and acerbic tongue. She married Congressman Nicholas Longworth in 1906 at the White House, bore her only child, a daughter, at forty-one, and became a grande dame of Washington society. She died in 1980 at the age of ninety-six.
Personal Notes: Alice had a bright, cheerful, sunny disposition. She played the piano, was an excellent tennis player, and loved games.
Death: Two days after giving birth to her daughter, the twenty-two-year-old Alice died of Bright's disease (kidney failure) complicated by the birth. Roosevelt held her while she died and was further saddened when his mother died the same day. Seized by a great depression, he left little Alice with his sister and fled to his ranch in the Dakota territory. He never spoke of Alice again, even to his daughter. He wrote about her once a year after her death and did not mention her in his autobiography.

SARAH JANE FULKS FUTTERMAN REAGAN KARGER (aka JANE WYMAN)
(1914–)

The Straight Facts

Born: January 4, 1914
Birthplace: St. Joseph, Missouri
Ancestry: German, English
Physical Characteristics: 5'5" tall, 125 lbs., brown hair, brown eyes
Religion: Roman Catholic
Husbands: (1) Myron Futterman
　　　　　　(2) Ronald Reagan (1911–)
　　　　　　(3) Fred Karger
　　　　　　(4) Fred Karger

Dates of Marriages: (1) 1937–1938
(2) 1940–1948
(3) 1952–1955
(4) 1961–1966
Places of Marriages: (1) New Orleans, Louisiana
(2) Glendale, California
(3) Los Angeles, California
(4) Los Angeles, California
Children: One son, two daughters

The More Colorful Facts

Astrological Sign: Capricorn
Childhood and Family Life: Sarah Jane Fulks is the youngest child of Richard Fulks, a public official in St. Joseph, Missouri, and his second wife, Emma Reise. There have been rumors that she was adopted and that in later years she changed both the date and year of her birth. She has made no public statement to substantiate or discredit either claim. She attended schools in St. Joseph and set out for California in the early 1930s after graduation from high school.
Hollywood Career: At eighteen, Sarah Jane made her screen debut dancing in the chorus of Busby Berkeley's shows. In 1936, she changed her name for professional purposes to Jane Wyman. The suggestion was made by her agent, William Demerest (who would later turn actor and become more well known as Uncle Charlie on TV's "My Three Sons"). She became a contract player for Warner Bros. and would appear in more than eighty movies. She was typecast in flamboyant and usually comic roles, as a wisecracking chorus girl or the best friend. (See the following list.)
Courtship and Marriage: Jane Wyman met fellow contract player Ronald Reagan while shooting publicity stills. They carried on a three-year courtship discreetly and clandestinely because she was in the process of divorcing her first husband and to stave off gossip. In 1939, both accompanied columnist Louella Parsons on her nationwide tour where their romance blossomed. Both admit Jane was the agressor at first. He proposed on the set of *Brother Rat.* They were married on January 24, 1940, at the Wee Kirk o'Heather Church. The reception was at the home of Louella Parsons and they honeymooned briefly in Palm Springs. For her ensemble, the twenty-six-year-old bride wore a floor length, high-necked, long-sleeved blue satin gown. Instead of a veil, she wore a dark fur hat and carried a matching fur muff. She also wore a fifty-two-carat amethyst engagement ring.

Children: Jane and Reagan had three children. Maureen Elizabeth, who was born in 1941, has been married three times and has been a reporter, actress, and political activist. Son Michael was adopted in 1945, has been married twice, has two children, and has been a businessman, race driver, and author. A second daughter died after a few hours of birth in 1947.

Divorce: During their marriage, each continued to work and raise the children. They purchased a home in Los Angeles and a ranch in the San Fernando Valley called Yearling Row after their two best films, *The Yearling* (hers) and *King's Row* (his). As their careers took different paths and Reagan became more politically minded, the two drifted apart. In May 1948, Jane filed for divorce which was finalized on July 18, 1949. Showing a great deal of class and decorum, when asked about her former husband the politician, her usual comment has been "... we are good friends and one does not talk about their former spouses."

Other Marriages: Like her birthdate and parentage, rumors persist of a failed teenage marriage to a Eugene Wyman. Whether or not she married him is supposition, but she did adopt the name Wyman when she came to Hollywood. Her first acknowledged marriage was to dress manufacturer Myron Futterman in 1937. The marriage lasted only a few months and they divorced in December 1938. After divorcing Reagan, she nearly married attorney Greg Bautzer in 1951, and had a three-week engagement to building contractor Travis Kleefeld, twelve years her junior, in 1952. Eight months later, she eloped with bandleader Fred Karger, divorcing him in 1955. They remarried in 1961 but again divorced in 1966.

Personal Notes: Jane plays the piano, a good game of golf, and is a passable painter. In Hollywood during the thirties and forties, she was known as a "nightclubber," frequenting the Trocadero and Coconut Grove. An astute businesswoman, she handles many details of her investments and career. In the 1950s, she converted to Catholicism and is active in church affairs. Jane also is a volunteer for many charitible events, most notably the Arthritis Foundation. She also claims to have always been a registed Republican.

Post-Divorce Career: Following her divorce from Reagan, she continued to act. She embarked on a singing career following a movie with Bing Crosby. In 1954, she won an Academy Award for *Johnny Belinda.* In the 1960s she had her own television show "The Jane Wyman Show." She continued acting, and in 1981, began a new TV series, "Falcon Crest."

HOSTESSES

For a variety of reasons, women other than First Ladies or wives have served as official hostesses for a president. The First Lady may have been unable to officiate or the president was not married or was widowed. This section features some of the more prominent of these hostesses.

THE JEFFERSON SISTERS

MARTHA WASHINGTON (PATSY) JEFFERSON RANDOLPH (1772–1836) was the oldest of the six Jefferson children. Only ten when her mother died, she first lived with her Carr cousins and then the Eppes cousins. When Thomas Jefferson went to France as peace commissioner in 1784, she sailed with him on the SS *Ceres*. While in Paris, she attended l'Abbaye Royale de Penthemonte. For years, the most elite of the young French misses attended this school, including Adrienne de Noailles, the future Marquise de Lafayette, and Hortense de Beauharnais, step-daughter of Napoleon Bonaparte and the future queen of Holland.

Tall, red-haired, freckled Patsy was devoted to her father. She was a good horsewoman, fluent in French, could dance, play the harpsichord, and was very nearsighted. She was quite upset that Jefferson only allowed her to spend three evenings a week partying. At one of these parties, she became reacquainted with her third cousin, Thomas Mann Randolph, Jr.

Randolph (1768–1828), a recent graduate of the University of Edinburgh, would go on to Congress and serve as governor of Virginia. They were married in 1790 at Monticello by the Rev. Mr. Maury and had twelve children. All the sons were named after prominent Americans. Eighth child James Madison Randolph was the first child to be born in the White House. The Randolphs divided their time between Monticello, his father's estate, Edgehill, and their own estate, Varina.

During Jefferson's presidency, they lived almost exclusively in the White House. Patsy hosted public receptions and entertained in the French tradition. She also assisted Dolley Madison in the receiving and returning of calls. Her diary relates an amusing afternoon where she made calls dressed in Dolley's cloak and using Dolley's name, so the latter could spend a day off with her husband.

Jefferson became more attached to her in retirement, and Patsy was his nearly constant companion. She died of apoplexy (stroke) at Edgehill estate in 1836 and is buried at Monticello. Her portrait by Joseph Boze is hung in the State Department building.

MARY (POLLY) JEFFERSON EPPES (1778–1804) was only four when her mother died. She was sent to live with her aunt, Elizabeth Eppes, when her father and Patsy went to France. Jefferson repeatedly pleaded for her to join him but she refused and became hysterical whenever the subject was mentioned. Jefferson finally resorted to having her shanghaied on a mail-boat to England, accompanied only by her maid (and half-aunt) Sally Hemings. It was a bewildered eight-year-old who was met at the dock by Abigail Adams, the wife of the American ambassador, who cared for her until Jefferson could come for her.

Maria Jefferson Eppes

Once in Paris, she attended the same school as her sister. As French was the only language spoken, she became known as Marie, but upon her return to America, she changed it to Maria, by which name she was known for the rest of her very short life.

She married childhood playmate and cousin John "Jack" Wayles Eppes (1773–1823). Eppes would serve in Congress and the Senate. Like her mother and sister, Maria followed the family tradition of marrying a cousin. The Eppeses had three children. Maria had only one "season" in Washington, leaving most duties to her sister.

She died at age twenty-six of complications from childbirth; she is buried in the family vault at Monticello.

THE JACKSON HOSTESSES

Andrew Jackson was a recent widower when he took office in in 1829. He asked his wife's niece to serve as his hostess. When his adopted son married in 1831, he asked his son's wife to serve as hostess of the Hermitage.

EMILY DONELSON (1808–1836) married Andrew Jackson Donelson, son of Rachel's brother John, at age seventeen. The brown-eyed, auburn-haired beauty attended the Old Academy School in Nashville. Married at the Hermitage, the couple lived at Tulip Grove, a cottage on the grounds.

Nicknamed "Lovely Emily," Jackson called her "my daughter." She had a difficult time keeping order in a White House of backwoodsmen, old soldiers, and politicians. People's president Jackson wanted it to be a people's house. Emily greeted guests dressed in American calico, which was the trademark of those who supported the Jackson cause.

The Donelsons had four children, all of whom were born at the White House and had presidential godparents; Jackson for two, Martin Van Buren and James K. Polk, one each. One son would die for the Confederacy at Chickamauga.

Emily Donelson

After refusing Jackson's orders to recognize Peggy Eaton, the wife of the secretary of war, Emily was banished to the Hermitage until the Eatons left Washington in 1831. Emily returned to Washington where she resumed her hostess duties. She died at age twenty-eight of tuberculosis. A portrait of Emily by Ralph E.W. Earl hangs in the Queen's Bedroom in the White House.

SARAH YORKE JACKSON (1805–1887) was the daughter of Peter Yorke of Philadelphia. She married the legally adopted son of Andrew Jackson, Andrew Jackson, Jr., in 1831. They spent most of the time overseeing the Hermitage estate. She served as White House hostess only after Emily died. Sarah and Andrew had five children, two of whom served in the Confederacy. She is buried with her husband at the Hermitage.

ANGELICA SINGLETON VAN BUREN

Angelica Van Buren

ANGELICA SINGLETON VAN BUREN (1816–1878) was the youngest daughter of South Carolinian planter Richard Singleton and Mary Coles. She attended the finest schools, including Madame Grelaud's Seminary in Philadelphia. The family was well connected on both sides with relatives in the Senate and in the State Department.

In the summer of 1838, she paid an extended visit to her uncle, Senator William Preston, in Washington. Cousin Dolley Madison arranged a private reception for her at the White House. Matchmaker Dolley was sure there would be an attraction between Angelica, and the widowed president or one of his four sons. Six months later, Angelica married Major Abraham Van Buren (1807–1873), a West Point graduate and private secretary to his father. The happy father of the groom, Martin Van Buren, asked his new daughter-in-law to serve as his hostess.

The blue-eyed, black-haired beauty made her debut as hostess on January 1, 1839, at the annual New Year's reception. Dressed all in white, she wore three ostrich plumes in her hair to make her appear taller. She also created a fashion craze in Washington by being among the first to wear hoop skirts.

She and Abraham took a delayed honeymoon to Europe in the spring of 1839. They were popular at European courts and the multilingual Angelica charmed all she met. The highlight of the trip was a private audience with young Queen Victoria.

Returning to Washington, she tried to adopt European customs and was severly criticized for it. She was not a popular hostess; her receptions were considered too royal and aristocratic.

She died in 1878 in New York City. Her White House portrait was painted by Henry Inman and hangs in the Red Room. Jacqueline Kennedy claimed Angelica's portrait was her favorite of all First Ladies in the White House collection.

HARRISON'S DAUGHTER-IN-LAW

Jane Irwin Harrison

JANE FINDLAY IRWIN HARRISON (1804–1846) was the daughter of Archibald Irwin and Mary Ramsey. One of her sisters married John Scott Harrison and was the mother of twenty-third president Benjamin Harrison.

She married William Henry Harrison, Jr. in 1824. The younger Harrison was a lawyer who died in 1838, at age thirty-eight, leaving Jane a widow with two sons. The eldest son married the daughter of a John Kennedy of Ireland.

Jane accompanied father-in-law William Henry Harrison to Washington because her mother-in-law had influenza and was forbidden to travel for three months. She and the aunt for which she was named, Jane Findlay, had just begun to set the White House in order when Harrison died of pneumonia, thirty-one days into his term. They did no entertaining on their own but did attend the inaugural ball.

They accompanied the president's body back to North Bend, Ohio. Jane died there, five years later at age forty-two. Her official portrait hangs in the William Henry Harrison home in Vincennes, Indiana.

THE TYLER BRIDES

Priscilla Cooper Tyler

(ELIZABETH) PRISCILLA COOPER TYLER was born on June 14, 1816 in New York City to British tragedian Thomas Abthorpe Cooper and Mary Fairlee. She was the third of nine children, had dark brown hair, and was quite beautiful. She made her stage debut at the age of three. Her first starring role was in *Virginius* in 1834, a tragedy by Sheridan Knowles.

She met Robert Tyler (1816–1877) while he was a law student. They were married in 1839 at St. James Episcopal Church in Bristol, Pennyslvania; John Tyler served as his son's best man. They had nine children, including a daughter who was born at the White House.

A charming and gracious hostess, she captivated both men and women. In 1843, she hosted a birthday party for one of her daughters, and the only adult invited was Dolley Madison. Pregnant with her second child, she grew ill at a White House party, fainted, and was caught by Daniel Webster

A frantic Robert poured a pitcher of water over them in an attempt to revive her, and Webster had to be dried off before leaving. She was happy to turn her duties over to her new stepmother, Julia, in 1844.

Sympathetic to the Southern cause, they moved to Montgomery, Alabama. Robert would serve as a Confederate treasury official and later as editor of the *Montgomery Mail and Advertiser*. She died at age seventy-three in Montgomery.

LETITIA (LETTY) TYLER SEMPLE (1821–1907) was the fourth of eight children of John Tyler and his first wife, Letitia Christian. Little is known about her life, but she did share hostess duties. She married James Semple in 1839; they had no children. She deeply resented her stepmother, and it was many years before she reconciled with her father. She died in 1907 at the age of eighty-nine.

MISS BETTY

Mary Elizabeth Taylor Bliss

MARY ELIZABETH "BETTY" TAYLOR BLISS (1824–1909) was the youngest of Zachary Taylor's daughters. She was educated at a Philadelphia finishing school. Margaret Taylor was a semi-invalid who handled all administrative duties but delegated social functions to Betty.

At age twenty-five, she married Lt. Colonel William Wallace Smith Bliss (1815–1853). Entering West Point at age thirteen, he was nicknamed "Perfect" by the men in his regiment. Bliss was an aide to his father-in-law and later became confidential secretary. He died in 1853 of yellow fever while crossing Panama. His place in the regiment was taken by fellow West Point graduate, Ulysses S. Grant.

Betty was a popular hostess, with charm and grace. For the inaugural ball, she wore a simple white dress and a single white flower in her hair. She was often called the "Wild Rose of the White House."

After leaving the White House, she married Virginian Philip Pendleton Dandridge. They were sympathetic to the Southern cause and were loyal to former brother-in-law Jefferson Davis. She died at age eighty-five in 1909 and had no children by either marriage. A daguerreotype of Betty by J. E. McClees belongs to the Smithsonian.

VARINA ANNE BANKS HOWELL DAVIS

VARINA ANNE BANKS HOWELL DAVIS (1826–1906) was the daughter of William Burr Howell and Margaret Louisa Kempe. Her paternal grandfather was a governor of New Jersey. She was born at her maternal grandfather's plantation in Marengo, Louisiana, and was the second of eleven children. She was taught at home by Judge George Winchester, who was a major influence in her life.

She was seventeen when she met widower Jefferson Finis Davis (1808–1889) when he visited his sister's home for Christmas. After a eighteen month courtship they were married in 1845 at her parents' home, called the Briers, outside of Natchez, Mississippi. The nineteen-year-old bride wore a white embroidered muslin gown with touches of lace. She wore a single rose in her dark hair. After the ceremony, they left for Washington as Davis was a member of Congress.

For the next fifteen years they were active politically and socially in Washington. When Davis's former in-laws, the Taylors, lived in the White House (Davis's first wife Sarah Knox Taylor died of malaria after three months of marriage), they were frequent guests. When Davis's friend Franklin Pierce was elected president, he invited the West Point graduate to serve as his secretary of war. Mrs. Pierce was a semi-invalid and Pierce asked Varina to officiate at select functions. Most entertaining was done at the Davis home and not the White House as Varina did not want to usurp the role of First Lady. She felt sorry for Jane Pierce and often took her infant son to visit the childless First Lady. Jane found great comfort from the child and soon began to be seen in public again.

Varina also unconsciously started the First Lady on the road toward assuming her role as hostess. Jane began to hear stories of how popular and gay the parties had been at the Davis home and became quite jealous. Her appearances were few, but at least she began to come out of her shell.

At the start of the Civil War, the Davises left Washington and returned to their home. When Davis was elected president of the Confederacy, they moved first to Mobile, Alabama, and then to Richmond, Virginia. Varina played her role as hostess with charm and grace. The Confederacy's defeat saw the entire Davis family (father, mother, and four children) hunted by federal troops. They were finally caught, although Varina had tried to hide her husband by throwing a large poncho over him. This gave rise to the rumors that Davis had tried to escape by dressing as a woman.

The family was taken to prison and its goods confiscated, even the baby's clothes. Davis was thrown into a separate prison Varina petitioned to live with him and this request was granted. When Davis was released from prison in 1868, they lived in New York. After Davis's death in 1889, Varina continued to be a symbol of the South, and always signed her name Mrs. V. Jefferson Davis. She wrote articles for Joseph Pulitzer and traveled. She met Julia Grant in 1893 and they became great friends. Julia invited Varina to attend the dedication ceremonies at Grant's Tomb and she accepted.

She died at age eighty in New York's Majestic Hotel. With much pomp and circumstance, she was laid to rest next to her husband in Richmond's Hollywood Cemetery.

THE DEMOCRATIC QUEEN

James Buchanan was the only president who never married. He asked his niece and ward, HARRIET REBECCA LANE, to serve as his First Lady.

Harriet was born on May 9, 1830, in Mercersburg, Pennsylvania. She was the sixth of seven children of Jane Buchanan (1793–1839) and Irishman Elliott Tole Lane (1784–1840). When she was orphaned at the age of ten, Buchanan became her guardian and supervised her education. Among the schools that turned the gangly young girl into a refined lady was the Academy of Visitation in Georgetown, from which she was graduated in 1848.

"Hal" accompanied "Nunc" to England when he became ambassador to the Court of St. James's in 1853. Blonde, violet-eyed Harriet charmed those at the British court. Queen Victoria conferred on her the rank of ambassador's wife, the first time that honor was awarded to a lady not married to an ambassador.

Entering the White House, she went about refurbishing the home, which had been neglected during the Pierce years. She bought American-made furniture and had a conservatory built so there would always be a fresh supply of flowers available, with roses being her favorite. She officiated during difficult times as the rift was growing between North and South and it was difficult to remain neutral. Two major social events occurred during her tenure.

Harriet Lane

The first was the visit of the Prince of Wales, the future Edward VII. It was the first visit by a member of the royal family to the former colonies and the prince had been traveling incognito as Baron Renfrew. A grand reception was held for the prince, who stayed at the White House as the guest of the president. He slept in Buchanan's room, while Buchanan slept on a couch in the hall. Buchanan was careful to remove Harriet's picture from his room so there would be no question of impropriety.

The second event was a reception honoring the Japanese diplomatic mission, also first-time visitors to the country. Harriet and cabinet wives were presented to the ministers in flowing silk robes. They were the only ladies the Japanese considered worthy of meeting.

Hal was said to be warm, charming, and kindhearted. She was called the "Great Mother of the Indians" for her work at improving their living conditions. Buchanan would not allow her to accept any gifts, believing it would show partiality to the giver. One gift piano-player Harriet did not have to return was a piece of music written for her called "Listen to the Mocking Bird." Written by Septimus Winner under the psuedonym Alice Hawthorne in 1855, it was dedicated to her. The cutter SS *Harriet Lane* was commissioned in 1857. According to Coast Guard records, the first naval shots in the Civil War were fired from this vessel. A second cutter named for her was commissioned by the wife of Transportation Secretary Drew Lewis in 1982.

Five years after leaving the White House, thirty-five-year-old Harriet married Baltimore banker Henry Elliott Johnston at Buchanan's Wheatland home. The Rev. Dr. Edward Young Buchanan (1811–1897), Buchanan's younger brother, performed the January 11, 1866 ceremony. (Rev. Buchanan was married to the sister of composer Stephen Foster.) The newlyweds spent their honeymoon in Cuba. It was a happy but tragic marriage. They had two sons who died in infancy and Johnston himself died an early death.

In her widowhood, Harriet was very involved in philanthropic work. She organized the Choir School of the Cathedral of Saints Peter and Paul in Washington, D.C. The Harriet Lane Home for Invalid Children was founded at Johns Hopkins University thanks to her contributions. In her will, one-half of her fine arts collection went to Johns Hopkins and the rest to the Smithsonian, which became the nucleus for the National Gallery of Art.

Harriet died in 1906 at the age of seventy-six of heart failure. She is buried next to her family in Greenmount Cemetery in Baltimore. Her portrait by John Henry Brown hangs in the National Gallery of Art.

THE JOHNSON SISTERS

MARTHA JOHNSON PATTERSON (1828–1901) was the oldest of the five Johnson children. As Eliza was a semi-invalid, the duties of hostess fell to her two daughters. Martha was no stranger to Washington, having been a frequent visitor to the Polk White House while a student at the Academy of Visitation in Georgetown.

Blonde Martha was said to closely resemble her father. Using an appropriation of $30,000, she redecorated the mansion after the wear and tear of the war years. Slipcovers and a liberal use of flowers helped hide scars on other items. Monday afternoons the sisters received guests. There was no pause in entertaining during the impeachment trial of their father. Johnson may have been politically unpopular, but his administration was very successful socially.

In 1885, Martha married David Trotter Patterson (1818–1891), judge of the circuit court of Tennessee and later senator. They had two children, who were raised just as if they were home in Greeneville. Martha even milked the family cow on the White House lawn. She died at age seventy-three and is buried at the Andrew Johnson National Cemetery.

MARY JOHNSON STOVER (1832–1883) was four years her sister's junior. A widow when Johnson became president, she cared for her mother

Martha Johnson Patterson

while Martha attended to social affairs. Very fashion conscious, she and her sister usually dressed in flattering styles.

First husband Col. Daniel Stover (1826–1864) was killed during the Civil War and left her with three young children. Second husband William Ramsey Brown was a widower whose first wife was a second cousin of Abraham Lincoln. They divorced in 1886 after seven years of marriage.

Mary died at age fifty-one and is also buried at the Andrew Johnson National Cemetery.

MARY ARTHUR MCELROY

Chester Arthur had been a widower for 1½ years when he ascended to the presidency in 1881. Daughter Nell, at age ten, was much too young to assume the duties of White House hostess. He enlisted the aid of his youngest sister, MARY ARTHUR MCELROY, wives of friends, and former First Ladies Julia Tyler, Harriet Lane Johnston, Julia Grant, and Lucy Hayes to assist as he was well known for his lavish entertainments.

For four months of the year, Mary would leave her home in Albany and travel to Washington. She supervised the running of the household and entertained guests. Schooled at Emma Willard's Seminary, she had married insurance man John Edward McElroy in 1861. She often brought her two daughters with her, and they and young Nell helped entertain guests. She gave weekly teas, lavish receptions, and was able to entice well-known musicians to perform at White House dinners.

After leaving the White House, Arthur and his children moved into

Mary Arthur McElroy

Mary's home, and when he died in 1886, she continued to raise the children. She died in 1916, leaving three children, five grandchildren, and six great-grand-children. A steel engraving of Mary by John Sartain is owned by the White House.

ROSE CLEVELAND

Grover Cleveland was a bachelor when he became president in 1885. He convinced youngest sister ROSE ELIZABETH to leave her teaching position at Houghton Academy, a fashionable girls school, to become his hostess. "Libbie" was a literary scholar who spoke several languages, including Greek. She earned more than $25,000 on her book entitled *George Elliott—Poetry and Other Studies.*

A firm believer in temperance, Libbie served no liquor or wines at her receptions and dinners. Her tables were set with imaginative menus, decorative plants, and flowers and wax sculptures. Each guest would find a rememberance of the event at his or her place setting, be it a festive ribbon, a pin, or boutonniére.

Rose Elizabeth Cleveland

She was only too glad to turn the duties over to new sister-in-law Frances in 1886. Libbie returned to her teaching duties. She died unmarried at age seventy-two in 1918, a victim of the influenza epidemic. Her official portrait is owned by the Smithsonian.

HOSTESSES REPRESENTED IN SMITHSONIAN DRESS COLLECTION

Martha Jefferson Randolph
Emily Donelson
Sarah Yorke Jackson
Angelica Van Buren
Jane Findlay Irwin Harrison
Mary Elizabeth (Betty) Bliss Dandridge
Harriet Lane Johnston
Martha Johnson Patterson
Mary Arthur McElroy

COMPARATIVE
DATA

The following data lists information about the wives of the presidents. A (w) denotes those wives who did not serve as First Lady.

First Ladies Who Lived into Their Nineties
Bess Truman

First Ladies Who Lived into Their Eighties
Dolley Madison
Anna Harrison
Sarah Polk
Lucretia Garfield
Mary Harrison (w)
Frances Cleveland
Edith Roosevelt
Helen Taft
Edith Wilson
Mamie Eisenhower

First Ladies Who Were Only Children
Ellen Arthur
Frances Cleveland
Grace Coolidge
Nancy Reagan

First Ladies Whose Birthplaces Are National Historic Sites
Abigail Adams
Mamie Eisenhower

First Ladies Whose Homes Are National Historic Sites
Eleanor Roosevelt

First Ladies Who Were Older Than Their Husbands
Martha Washington
Abigail Fillmore
Caroline Harrison
Florence Harding
Pat Nixon

First Ladies Who Were Widows When They Married
Martha Custis Washington
Martha Skelton Jefferson (w)
Dolley Todd Madison
Caroline McIntosh Fillmore (second Mrs. Millard Fillmore) (w)
Mary Dimmick Harrison (second Mrs. Benjamin Harrison) (w)
Edith Galt Wilson (second Mrs. Woodrown Wilson)

First Ladies Who Were Divorcees
Rachel Donelson Jackson (w)
Florence DeWolfe Harding
Betty Warren Ford
Sarah Jane Fulks (Wyman) "Futterman" Reagan (w)

First Ladies Who Attended the Inauguration of John F. Kennedy
Edith Wilson
Eleanor Roosevelt
Bess Truman
Mamie Eisenhower
Jacqueline Kennedy
Lady Bird Johnson
Pat Nixon
Betty Ford

First Ladies Who Married in Their Teens
Abigail Adams
Elizabeth Monroe
Eliza Johnson
Alice Roosevelt (w)
Mamie Eisenhower
Rosalynn Carter

First Ladies Who Married While Their Husbands Were President
Julia Tyler
Frances Cleveland
Edith Wilson

First Ladies Who Had No Children
Rachel Jackson (w)
Sarah Polk
Caroline Fillmore (w)
Edith Wilson

First Ladies Who Had Five or More Children
Abigail Adams
Martha Jefferson (w)
Anna Harrison
Letitia Tyler

Julia Tyler
Margaret Taylor
Eliza Johnson
Lucy Hayes
Lucretia Garfield
Frances Cleveland
Edith Roosevelt
Eleanor Roosevelt
Barbara Bush

First Ladies Who Celebrated Their Golden Wedding Anniversaries
Abigail Adams
Louisa Adams
Bess Truman
Mamie Eisenhower

First Ladies Whose Children Married in the White House
Eliza Monroe
Louisa Adams
Letitia Tyler
Julia Grant
Alice Roosevelt (w)
Ellen Wilson
Lady Bird Johnson
Pat Nixon

First Ladies Who Were Graduated From College
Lucy Hayes
Lucretia Garfield
Frances Cleveland
Grace Coolidge
Lou Hoover
Jacqueline Kennedy
Lady Bird Johnson
Pat Nixon
Rosalynn Carter
Nancy Reagan

First Ladies Who Taught School
Abigail Fillmore
Lucretia Garfield
Helen Taft

Ellen Wilson
Lou Hoover
Eleanor Roosevelt
Pat Nixon

First Ladies Awarded Franking Privileges by Congress
Martha Washington
Dolley Madison
Louisa Adams
Anna Harrison
Sarah Polk
Margaret Taylor
Mary Lincoln
Lucretia Garfield
Julia Grant
Frances Cleveland
Mary Harrison (w)
Ida McKinley
Edith Roosevelt
Edith Wilson
Florence Harding
Eleanor Roosevelt
Bess Truman
Mamie Eisenhower
Jacqueline Kennedy
Lady Bird Johnson

Members of the Daughters of the American Revolution
Julia Dent Grant
Caroline Harrison (first president general)
Mary Harrison (w)
Edith Roosevelt
Florence Harding
Eleanor Roosevelt (resigned)
Mamie Eisenhower
Rosalynn Carter (resigned)
Nancy Reagan
Barbara Bush

First Ladies Who Died in the White House
Letitia Tyler
Caroline Harrison
Ellen Wilson

First Ladies Represented in the Smithsonian Dress Collection

Martha Washington
Abigail Adams
Dolley Madison
Elizabeth Monroe
Louisa Adams
Julia Tyler
Sarah Polk
Abigail Fillmore
Jane Pierce
Mary Lincoln
Julia Grant
Lucy Hayes
Lucretia Garfield
Caroline Harrison
Frances Cleveland
Ida McKinley
Edith Roosevelt
Helen Taft
Ellen Wilson
Edith Wilson
Florence Harding
Grace Coolidge
Lou Hoover
Eleanor Roosevelt
Bess Truman
Mamie Eisenhower
Jacqueline Kennedy
Lady Bird Johnson
Pat Nixon
Betty Ford
Rosalynn Carter
Nancy Reagan

First Ladies Pictured on U.S. Postage Stamps

Martha Washington
Abigail Adams
Dolley Madison
Eleanor Roosevelt

First Ladies Pictured on U. S. Postal Cards

Martha Washington

Movie and Television Portrayals:

Martha Washington

Alexander Hamilton	1931	Gwendolin Logan
"First Ladies' Diaries"	1975 (TV)	Susan Browning
"George Washington"	1984 (TV)	Patty Duke Astin
"George Washington, II"	1986 (TV)	Patty Duke

Abigail Adams

1776	1972	Virginia Vestoff
"Land of the Free	1974 (TV)	Kate Wilkinson
"Adams Chronicles	1976 (TV)	Kathryn Walker
		Leora Dana
"American Woman: Portrait of Courage"	1976 (TV)	Joanna Miles
"George Washington"	1984 (TV)	Christine Estabrook

Martha Jefferson

1776	1972	Blythe Danner
"Patriots"	1976 (PBS)	Martha J. Brown
"Family Ties" (episode)	1985 (TV)	Meredith Baxter Birney

Dolley Madison

The Buccaneer	1938	Spring Byington
The Magnificent Doll	1946	Ginger Rogers

Louisa Adams

"Adams Chronicles"	1976 (TV)	Pamela Payton-Wright

Rachel Jackson

The Gorgeous Hussy	1936	Beulah Bondi
The President's Lady	1952	Susan Hayward
"First Ladies' Diaries"	1975 (TV)	Fran Brill

Mary Todd Lincoln

The Dramatic Life of Abraham Lincoln	1924	Nell Craig
Prisoner of Shark Island	1936	Leila McIntyre
The Plainsman	1936	Leila McIntyre
Young Mr. Lincoln	1939	Marjorie Weaver
Abe Lincoln in Illinois	1939	Ruth Gordon
Abraham Lincoln	1940	Ruth Gordon

"Abe Lincoln in Illinois"	1945 (TV)	Mary Michaels
Prince of Players	1955	Sarah Padden
"Abe Lincoln in Illinois"	1964 (TV)	Kate Reid
"Sandburg's Lincoln"	1974 (TV)	Michelle Marsh
		Sada Thompson
"The Last of Mrs. Lincoln"	1976 (TV)	Julie Harris
The Lincoln Conspiracy	1977	Frances Fordham
"The Blue and the Gray"	1982 (TV)	Janice Carroll
"Voyagers" (episode)	1983 (TV)	Rachel Bond
"Gore Vidal's Lincoln"	1988 (TV)	Mary Tyler Moore

Eliza Johnson
Tennessee Johnson	1942	Ruth Hussey

Julia Grant
"North and South, Book II"	1986 (TV)	Bonnie Bartlett

Lucretia Garfield
No More Excuses	1968	Linda Diesem

Frances Cleveland
Buffalo Bill and the Indians	1976	Shelley Duvall

Caroline Harrison
Stars and Stripes Forever	1952	Hellen Van Tuyl

Edith Roosevelt
"The Indomitable Theodore Roosevelt"	1985 (TV)	Philippa Roosevelt

Helen Taft
"Backstairs at the White House"	1979 (TV)	Julie Harris

Ellen Wilson
Wilson	1944	Ruth Nelson
"Backstairs at the White House"	1979 (TV)	Kim Hunter

Edith Wilson
Wilson	1944	Geraldine Fitzgerald
"First Ladies' Diaries"	1976 (TV)	Elizabeth Hubbard

"Backstairs at the White House"	1979 (TV)	Claire Bloom

Florence Harding

"Backstairs at the White House"	1979 (TV)	Celeste Holm

Grace Coolidge

"Backstairs at the White House"	1979 (TV)	Lee Grant

Lou Hoover

"Backstairs at the White House"	1979 (TV)	Jan Sterling

Eleanor Roosevelt

Sunrise At Campobello	1960	Greer Garson
"Eleanor and Franklin"	1976 (TV)	Hilary Stolla
		Tiffani Bol
		Shannon Terhune
		Mackenzie Phillips
		Jane Alexanor
"Eleanor and Franklin: The White House Years"	1977 (TV)	Jane Alexander
"Backstairs at the White House"	1979 (TV)	Eileen Heckert
Annie	1982	Lois de Banzie
"Eleanor, First Lady of the World"	1982 (TV)	Jean Stapleton
"Eleanor: In Her Own Words"	1987 (PBS)	Lee Remick

Bess Truman

"The Man from Independence"	1974 (TV)	June Drayton
"Collision Course"	1976 (TV)	Lucille Benson
"Backstairs at the White House"	1979 (TV)	Estelle Parsons

Mamie Eisenhower

"Backstairs at the White House"	1979 (TV)	Barbara Barrie
"Ike"	1979 (TV)	Bonnie Bartlett
"Kennedy"	1983 (TV)	Carmen Matthews

Jacqueline Kennedy

"Jacqueline Bouvier Kennedy"	1981 (TV)	Heather Hobbs "Jaclyn Smith
"Kennedy"	1983 (TV)	Blair Brown
"Robert Kennedy and His Times"	1984 (TV)	Juanin Clay
"LBJ"	1987 (TV)	Robin Curtis

Lady Bird Johnson

'Kennedy"	1983 (TV)	Tanny McDonald
"Robert Kennedy and His Times"	1985 (TV)	Danna Hanson
"LBJ"	1987 (TV)	Patti Lupone

Pat Nixon

"Blind Faith"	1979 (TV)	Cathleen Cordell
"The Final Days"	1989 (TV)	Susan Brown

Betty Ford

"The Betty Ford Story"	1987 (TV)	Gena Rowlands

Rosalynn Carter

"Saturday Night Live" (episode)	1978 (TV)	Laraine Newman

Nancy Reagan

"Saturday Night Live" (episode)	1986 (TV)	Terry Sweeney
"Saturday Night Live" (episode)	1989 (TV)	Jan Hooks

Barbara Bush

"Saturday Night Live" (episode)	1988 (TV)	Dennis Miller

INDEX

French Revolution, 17-18
Futterman, Myron, 177, 179

Gallela, Ron, 125
Galt, Norman, 83, 84
Garfield, James Abram, 30, 53, 58, 59-60
Garfield Lucretia Rudolph, 58-60, 198, 200, 201, 202, 204
Girl Scouts, 91, 98, 99
Golden Wedding Anniversaries, First Ladies who celebrated, 200
Gouvernor, Maria Hester Monroe, 17, 18
Grant, Frederick Dent, 51
Grant, Jesse Root, 52
Grant, Julia Boggs Dent, 50-53, 190, 193, 200, 201, 202, 204
Grant, Ulysses, Jr., 51-52
Grant, Ulysses Simpson, 50, 51, 53, 56, 188
Grilley, Patti Davis Reagan, 150

Habitat for Humanity, 146
Hagner, Belle, 74
Haig, Alexander, 153
"Hail to the Chief," 30
Hamilton, Alexander, 169
Hammersmith Farms, 121
Harding, Florence Mabel Kling De Wolfe, 88-91, 198, 199, 201, 202, 205
Harding, Warren Gamaliel, 79, 88, 89-91
Harrison, Anna Tuthill, 23-25, 198, 199, 201
Harrison, Benjamin, 24, 65, 66-67, 173, 174, 186
Harrison, Caroline Lavinia Scott, 65-67, 198, 201, 202, 204
Harrison, Elizabeth, 174
Harrison, Jane Findlay Irwin, 186-187, 195
Harrison, John Scott, 24, 25, 186
Harrison, Mary Scott Lord Dimmick, 173-174, 198, 201
Harrison, Russell, 66
Harrison, William Henry, 23, 24, 25, 67, 187
Harrison, William Henry, Jr., 186
Harry S. Truman Library and Museum, 109, 113
Hay, Eliza Monroe, 17, 18
Hayes, Birchard, 55
Hayes, Frances (Fanny), 56

Hayes, Lucy Ware Webb, 54-57, 74, 77, 193, 200, 202
Hayes, Rutherford Birchard, 54, 55-57, 77
Hayes, Rutherford (son), 55
Hayes, Scott, 55
Hayes, Webb Cook, 55
Hemings, Sally, 160, 182
Hermitage, 165, 183, 184
Hickock, Lorena, 107
Historic sites, First Ladies National birthplaces, 198 homes, 198
Hoover, Allan Henry, 97
Hoover, Herbert Charles, 97
Hoover, Herbert Clark, 75, 96, 97
Hoover, J. Edgar, 106
Hoover, Lou Henry, 96-100, 105, 200, 201, 202, 205
Hoover Presidential Library, 97, 100
Hopkins, Harry, 106
Hostesses, presidential, 180, 182-195
Howe, Louis, 105, 106
Hunter's Hill, 164
Hyde Park, 101, 103, 105, 108

Inaugural ball, first, 14
Iran hostage crisis, 146
Irving Washington, 38

Jackson, Andrew, 21, 162, 163-165, 183-184
Jackson, Andrew, Jr., 164, 184
Jackson, Rachel Donelson Robards, 162-165, 199, 203
Jackson, Sarah Yorke, 184, 195
"The Jane Wyman Show," 179
Jefferson, Lucy Elizabeth, 161
Jefferson, Martha Wayles Skelton, 160-161, 198, 199, 203
Jefferson, Thomas, 13, 160, 161, 182
JFK's inauguration, First Ladies who attended, 199
Jimmy Carter Presidential Center, 146
Johnny Belinda, 179
John Hopkins Medical School, 67, 192
Johnson, Andrew, 47, 48-49, 192
Johnson, Andrew, Jr., 48
Johnson, Charles, 48
Johnson, Claudia Alta Taylor (Lady Bird), 126-130, 135, 199, 200, 201, 202, 206
Johnson, Eliza McArdle, 47-49, 199, 200, 204,

ILLUSTRATION CREDITS